SILVER QUEEN

The Fabulous Story of Baby Doe Tabor

The Author

Caroline Bancroft was a third generation Coloradan who began her literary career by joining the staff of *The Denver Post* in 1928. For five years she edited a book page and wrote historical features for the Sunday edition. On a travel assignment for the *New York Evening Post*, she interviewed a long list of celebrated authors in New York, London, Paris, Holland, and India. Her articles have appeared in many nationally known magazines.

Her long-standing interest in western history was inherited. Her pioneer grandfather, Dr. F. J. Bancroft (after whom the three-crested, Continental Divide peak just south of James is named), was a founder of the Colorado Historical Society and its first president for seventeen years. Her father, George J. Bancroft, a mining engineer, wrote many mining and reclamation contributions to the growing body of Colorado lore.

Caroline Bancroft has carried on the family tradition. A Bachelor of Arts from Smith College, she later obtained a Master of Arts degree from the University of Denver, writing her thesis on Central City, Colorado. She taught Colorado history at Randell School in Denver and was the author of the intensely interesting series of Bancroft Booklets about Colorado, including *Unique Ghost Towns and Mountain Spots, Denver's Lively Past, Augusta Tabor, Tabor's Matchless Mine and Lusty Leadville, Famous Aspen, Six Racy Madams, The Unsinkable Mrs. Brown* and the extremely popular *Colorful Colorado*.

Edwin C. Johnson,
Governor of Colorado
1931-37, 1955-57

SILVER QUEEN

The Fabulous Story of
BABY DOE TABOR

CAROLINE BANCROFT

My Interest in Baby Doe

The formerly beautiful and glamorous Baby Doe Tabor, her millions lost many years before, was found dead on her cabin floor at the Matchless Mine in Leadville, Colorado, on March 7, 1935. Her body, only partially clothed, was frozen with ten days' stiffness into the shape of a cross. She had lain down on her back on the floor of her stove-heated one room home, her arms outstretched, apparently in sure foreboding that she was to die.

Newspapers and wires flashed the story to the world, telling the tragic end of the eighty-year-old recluse who had, during the decade of the 1880s, been one of the richest persons in the United States. Her body was found by a young woman, known to Leadville as Sue Bonnie (her real name was Naomi Pontiers), with whom Mrs. Tabor had been very sociable during the last three years of the older woman's life. Sue Bonnie had become concerned when she saw no smoke coming from her friend's cabin and had persuaded Tom French to break a way through three feet of snow from Little Stray Horse Gulch to Mrs. Tabor's lonely cabin on Fryer Hill. When the couple peered through the window, they discovered her prostrate form.

The once proud beauty was dead. Leadville, Denver, Central City and the world reacted immediately, producing a host of memories to round out the details of her extraordinary career. Other reminiscences came from Oshkosh, Wisconsin, where she was born, and from Washington, D. C., where she had married Tabor, President Arthur and several members of the cabinet in attendance at the wedding.

Her story had been a drama of contrasts, from rags to riches and from riches back to rags again, the whole play enacted against the backdrop of Colorado's magnificent and munificent mountains. But what those ruthless snow-capped peaks give, they also take away and almost as if they were gods, they single out certain characters in history to destroy by first making mad. Mrs. Tabor went to her death with a delusion about the Matchless Mine.

She had lived during the last years of her life largely through the charity of the citizens of Leadville and the company that held the mortgage on the Matchless. The mine had produced no ore in years and was not really equipped to work, although she could not find it in her soul to admit the harsh fact of reality. She dressed in mining clothes and off and on during the last twenty years made a pretense of getting out ore with a series of men she inveigled to work on shares. But she either quarreled with these partners when she became suspicious of their honesty or the men became disillusioned about the supposed fortune hidden in the Matchless and drifted off.

I only met her once, in the summer of 1927, when I called on her with my father, a mining engineer, who was making a swing around the state to report on the mining situation. Mrs. Tabor, who had known my father for

4

many years, showed us over the premises. She was polite to me but largely ignored me since she was concentrating on my father with the hope he might get her new backing.

The tiny cabin she lived in had been a former tool and machine shop of the Matchless and the actual hoisthouse was perhaps thirty feet or so away. When we entered the hoisthouse, it already had an aura of ghosts. Dirt and rust were accumulating from disuse and covered the hoist, cables and machinery that were still left there. It was my father's opinion, voiced to me as we drove off past the Robert E. Lee mine, that quite a lot of machinery had been stolen from the hoisthouse without her being aware of it. Or perhaps "the old lady," as he spoke of her, had sold it to get enough to eat and had forgotten the transaction in the forgetfulness of what mountaineers call "cabin fever," a strangeness that overtakes elderly people who live alone.

I was not so interested in the mining aspects of her situation as my father (who was always avid on the scent of ore—gold, silver, copper, tungsten, and at the end, rare minerals such as vanadium, molybdenum, uranium, titanium and tantalum). What interested me about Mrs. Tabor were her looks and her personality. I studied her quietly while she and my father talked about the glorious riches that would be uncovered if she "could just drift a little further north on the third level" or "sink a winze through to that stope on the fourth."

She was a little woman, very withered, and unattractively dressed in men's corduroy trousers, mining boots and a soiled, torn blouse. She had a blue bandana tied around her head and when we first drove up back of the Matchless, as close as the car could make it and started to walk to her cabin, she met us halfway, a very belligerent expression on her face. My father and she had not met in several years and it was not until after he gave his name that her manner changed.

She smiled then and said, "Why, of course, pray do forgive me. And what a beautiful daughter you have! It is my lasting sorrow that the Lord's work has taken my own daughter . . ."

I could not have been more startled. The smile, the manner, the voice and the flowery speech were anomalous in that strange figure. Her smile was positively, although very briefly, gay and flashing; the teeth, even and white and the voice, clear and bell-like, while the manner I can only describe as queenly despite her diminutive size.

I only remember two other things about that afternoon. After we had spent some time in the hoisthouse and walking about outside, while she and my father talked about the direction of veins and probable apexes, the price of silver and other matters not very interesting to my youthful ears, Father suggested that in the car he had a jug of homemade wine his housekeeper had made. It was during Prohibition and wine of any sort was a rarity so that when he invited her to have a drink for old time's sake, she seemed pleased and asked us up to the ledge to her cabin.

While Father went back to the car for the wine, she and I strolled on

5

ahead. I complimented her on the spectacular view of Mt. Massive and Mt. Elbert, two among three of Colorado's highest peaks, that we had had driving out Little Strayhorse Gulch.

She did not say anything but she turned her eyes full upon me, the only time I think that she looked directly at me. Again I was startled. They were very far apart and a gorgeous blue, their unusual color preserved through all the violence and drama and bitterness of her then seventy-two years.

Her cabin, really no more than a shack, was crowded with very primitive furniture, decorated with religious pictures, and stacked high in newspapers. It was quite neat although, to my mind, it could have stood a good dusting and the window panes had evidently not been washed since the winter snows. We drank our wine from an assortment of cups, one of them tin. She apologized for their not being very clean and said something about hauling her drinking water from some distance and using boiled mine water for other purposes.

I did not listen—to my shame, now. While they went on talking, I entertained myself with my own thoughts. I knew almost no Colorado history in those days; I had been out of the state for nine years at school, college and working in the East, my interests completely disassociated. To me, she was just one more of the queer mining characters my father knew, and he knew dozens. But I lived to regret my youthful ignorance and indifference.

At the time she died, I was in the East and two years later, the editor of *True Story* magazine commissioned me to write her biography, my fare being paid from New York to Colorado to do research for a five-part serial. I spent eight months in Leadville, Central City and Denver talking to old-timers, literally scores of them, who had known Baby Doe Tabor. I also looked up court records of Gilpin and Lake Counties and read old newspaper files. Through the years I have intermittently continued my study of Baby Doe, adding to my knowledge of her in the course of other researches. But for human interest details, my greatest source of information proved to be Sue Bonnie who had discovered Mrs. Tabor's body.

Sue Bonnie sold me the use of her name in order to meet the editorial requirements of *True Story* and in consequence, the original version of "Silver Queen," now very much altered, appeared from January to May of 1938, signed "Sue Bonnie." Of course, the serial was actually written by me, but through the publicity of that seeming authorship, she later became something of a town figure on her own. Sue Bonnie has since died.

This young woman had drifted into Leadville from New Haven, Connecticut, and had struck up an intimate friendship with Mrs. Tabor, apparently since the pretty Easterner reminded Mrs. Tabor of her dead daughter, Silver Dollar. The older woman had nicknamed the curly black-haired Sue, "Songbird," and it was their custom to visit back and forth two or three nights a week in each other's cabins, exchanging tales of dreams they had had, their probable meanings and writing down spiritualistic revelations they obtained from a ouija board.

Sue Bonnie gave me a large number of these papers written in a stubby pencil by Mrs. Tabor's hand and a scrap-book of hers pasted up spasmodically by the older woman. I, in turn, donated these documents to the Western History Department of the Denver Public Library where they may be viewed today by serious research workers. These papers are very helpful to an understanding of Baby Doe's character in its declining years.

But what was most revealing were the many reminiscences of the past which Mrs. Tabor chose to tell Sue Bonnie. Neither her friend nor I had any way of telling whether these many intimate memories of Baby Doe's were literally true. Sue Bonnie, who idolized her, believed every word and I, for my part, found in those instances where I could check what Baby Doe Tabor said against documentary evidence that they were substantially right.

I was never sure about Baby Doe's exact age; I thought she had tampered with it—and I said so in the first editions of this booklet. Oshkosh readers interested themselves in my problem. They established the fact that for Colorado consumption she had taken six years off her age and had arranged a middle name for a more pleasing and romantic effect. I still hope to journey to Oshkosh sometime to personally thank residents there for copies of her christening, her wedding and other important documents. In 1953, the Colorado Historical Society opened to research workers letters and scrapbooks in their possession, unavailable for eighteen years after her death, so that a definitive biography may finally be written.

But in whatever form it is presented, popular or scholarly, Baby Doe's story has an astonishing vitality. Her name is as imperishable as the mountains she chose to live in for the greater part of her life. Her cabin in Leadville was for many years torn at and carved upon by souvenir-hunting tourists. Finally, it was a desolate ruin, until, in 1953, I spearheaded a civic movement to restore the cabin and open it as a tourist attraction. The cabin is now an almost exact replica of the home she lived in. Also, some of the fragile gold furniture and jewel box, salvaged from her heyday, may be seen at the Teller House in Central City. Until 1958 her famous suite could be seen at the Windsor Hotel in Denver, and her wedding dress and other Tabor relics are on exhibit at the Colorado Historical Museum. She is immortal.

So let us have Baby Doe Tabor tell us of her life in nearly her own words —many she actually used in talking to Sue Bonnie and others I have imagined as consonant with her character and the facts of her story.

Chapter One

"Oh, you are too beautiful to work, my lovely Bessie. I want you to keep your arms always as exquisite as they are now. Never spoil those curves!"

I can remember my mother pushing me away from a scrub-board with these words when I was a girl. It was in the kitchen of our home in Oshkosh, Wisconsin, just before the great fires of 1874 and 1875. Papa was still quite rich, even though he had been badly hit in the horrible fire of 1859. Later he was nearly ruined by these last ones which practically destroyed our whole town twice in little more than a year. Mama was a darling. She had a gay, uncomplaining disposition, although she bore fourteen children and life was far from easy for her. She was very good to all us children but I think, in some ways, I was her favorite of the eleven who grew up.She always said she wanted me to have all the things she had missed and little did we think, then, how fabulously and how violently her wish would be fulfilled.

My parents were Irish and were very good Catholics. Before· St. Peter's Church was erected in 1850, divine services were held in our home since my father, Peter McCourt, was a good friend of Father Bonduel. Father Bonduel was the first missionary priest of that wild lumber country. He had spent twelve years with the Indians of Lake Poygan before he came to Oshkosh, and his spirit was an inspiring one.

All Father Bonduel's adventures had happened, of course, many years before I was born. But so fond were Mama and Papa of him that when I came along, the fourth child, they were still talking about him while I was growing up. He died when I was seven years old, but I liked the stories about him so much that I changed my middle name from Nellis to Bonduel, later on. I was christened Elizabeth Nellis McCourt (which was Mama's name) at St. Peter's on Oct. 7, 1854, when I was twelve days old. My religion, so begun, was to stand me in good stead as the years rolled by with their extraordinary story.

"Too beautiful to work!"

I'm afraid that phrase helped to make me vain, and I already had the upright pride natural to all us McCourts. But there were lots of other things besides vanity and pride instilled into me as I was maturing, too. I would not for the world want to reflect on the bringing-up Papa and Mama gave me. They were truly fine people, respected and admired by the conservative members of the community.

Oshkosh, in those days, was a very lively, up-and-coming town. It had been called after Chief Oshkosh, a famous Indian of the Butte des Morts district, whose name in Menominee speech means "brave." And certainly no town was more brave. It had every grandeur of bravery—the swaggering bravery of the frontier and the spiritual bravery of people who have great faith.

The swaggering frontier bravery was all around. It resounded in the dangerous felling of pines, the perilous running of logs, the great lumber barges with their snarling bargemen floating through the middle of the town into beautiful Lake Winnebago. Seventeen sawmills, six shingle mills, and three planing mills buzzed and whirred constantly. In these, many friends and acquaintances were amassing great lumber fortunes.

Today the forests have been cut back into the northern part of the state. But at that time Oshkosh was at the outlet of the Wolf pinery. Log runners, tree cutters, millers, shippers—lumbermen of all sorts came into Oshkosh for a good time, with their wages or their pile, and many remained to build homes and settle down. They were a devil-may-care, hearty lot, ruddy-skinned and robust. Hardly any foreigners were among them. Mostly they were enterprising young Americans who had come from farther East to grow up in a new country. Their masculine bravery made a great impression on a young girl's heart.

The spiritual bravery of the place was also magnificent. When I was nineteen and twenty we had those two terrific fires in the town which practically destroyed it. Papa had a clothing and custom-tailoring store at 21 Main street. It was from McCourt & Cameron that most of the fashionable men of the town bought their suits and accessories. I liked to hang around the store to watch them drive up in their smart buggies and toss the reins to a hitching-post boy Papa hired. Nearly always they would stop at the counter before going to the fitting rooms at the rear and say:

"Beautiful daughter you have there, Mr. McCourt—aren't you afraid someone will steal her?"

I thought this much more fun than associating with girls my own age, and when the first fire started I was, as usual, down at the store. It began up the street, and since all the buildings were frame, spread rapidly. I ran home with the news.

"Mama, our store's on fire!" I yelled at the top of my lungs as soon as I got home. Our house was a palatial one on Division street easily to be compared with the fine residences on stately oak-lined Algoma boulevard. We even kept a maid of all work—but these good days were soon to pass. July 14, 1874, was a fatal day.

Mama came running out on the verandah, and the expression on her face was dreadful. Up to that moment I had only thought of the excitement of it all. But when I saw her horror and dismay I realized the danger. Perhaps Papa would be killed fighting the fire—or if he lived through it, he might not have enough money to build a new store and stock it. All sorts of awful thoughts ran through my head and they were true forebodings. We lost both our store and our lovely house in this disaster.

So did lots of other brave people. It seems impossible when I think of it now. But there were actually seven hundred structures—houses, barns, and places of business that had to be rebuilt that summer. The smell of new lumber, which goodness knows we were used to in Oshkosh, now came from our own front yards. Since our house was lost, we went to stay with more fortunate friends of Mama's until we could re-build. We had our lumber delivered to their yard so that it wouldn't be stolen. It was all very exciting.

"Frontier courage," Mama said.

"Faith," Papa contradicted, because he believed everything that happened was God's will.

The hammering, banging and shouting that summer were terrific. The noise and energy made a deep impression on me. My brothers and I would walk around and watch the bustling, stimulating activity. It was one of the most delightful vacations I ever spent. That year I didn't go down to the waterfront as much as I generally did, to watch the steamers hauling fleets of logs and timbers. I didn't bother to see the graceful yachts of the Oshkosh Yacht Club go skimming out over the broad blue waters of the lake toward Calumet County on the eastern shore. I just watched the carpentry sideshows along Main Street.

It was the next spring that brought final tragedy to Papa's fortunes. He and his partner had just got a store re-built and running again when the Lord's chastisement fell once more. It was a windy spring day, April 28, 1875, that another fire broke out, this time in Morgan's mill. Papa had been home to dinner and it was just past one o'clock when I was shepherding my younger brothers and sister, Claudia, back to school. As we started down the street a lumberman on a horse came galloping up.

"We need every able-bodied man down by Fox River. Fire in Morgan's mill," he yelled to Papa.

We all climbed into the buggy and set off at a fast trot. The tugs slapped the horses' flanks as we all but flew down hill in the violent wind. When we drew onto Jackson Drive, enormous flying cinders were shooting from Morgan's mill and floating across to some lumber piles. The scene was unbelievably beautiful, but there was a note of desperation in Papa's voice:

"We're done for in this wind—"

He was right. Roaring and crackling, the lumber piles by the river went up in flames like match-boxes. Immediately the street became bedlam. Everybody tore towards their stores to try to save their stocks of goods. Breathless, terror-stricken, we ran behind Papa toward our own store, where he and his partner, Mr. Cameron, loaded us with goods to stow in the buggy. All Main street was wild. Someone rushed up and tried to grab our team's bridles and lead them off. I was just coming out of the door with a bolt of brown suiting.

"Hey, there!" I yelled, dropping the bolt and making a dive for the buggy whip.

The man ducked and dashed off. Before I knew what was happening something thundered by and knocked me down. Luckily I wasn't hurt. As I started to cry out in protest, I saw it was a crazed horse with no bridle that someone had let loose from the livery stable a few doors down.

Beyond, pandemonium was rampant everywhere. The whole town was trying to save something, seizing any sort of empty vehicle or cart and piling stuff in. The board walk was alive with jostling crowds, fighting their way in and out of the stores. Careening teams in the street broke away from their drivers and ran away from the fire, some of them overturning their wagons as they fled. Luckily, we were able to hold our team still, and after the buggy was filled with goods, we unfastened the tugs and hitched the horses to a buckboard we found abandoned in the street. Papa and Mr. Cameron filled it and drove off. Grasping the tongue of the buggy, we young McCourts were able to haul it slowly up Main Street away from danger. The spreading fire blazed fiercely, and near us walls were falling.

The flames took only twenty minutes to race from Morgan's mill to the Milwaukee and St. Paul depot and freight station. We had hoped the fire would turn back toward the river, but it was becoming evident that it wouldn't. After our store caught and we had carted away what goods we could, we went back as near as we dared to watch the terrific holocaust.

"Oh, I can't bear it!" I wailed as I began to realize the extent of the destruction before my eyes.

The Harding Opera House was starting to go. Flames from the large windows of the Temple of Honor and its projecting wooden balcony were leaping out and licking my favorite building, the Opera House. In the midst of the noise and confusion I got separated from the rest of the family and just stood, numb and helpless, my eyes filling with tears. The Opera House was a symbol to me—it made my secret ambition to be an actress seem more than a dream—and I had had thrilling afternoons there enjoying matinees of the many road companies as well as at our own McCourt Hall, which had been the theatrical center before the Opera House was built. Now both were going—

I put my hands up to my eyes to shut out the sight. But the roar in my ears remained, and was just as heart-rending. Fascinated as if by a spell, I uncovered my eyes and stared. I couldn't move. After hardly burning at all, the walls of the Opera House collapsed with a terrifying rumble that made the ground tremble. Thudding bricks rolled near me. The terrific heat at its sides had been too much for the great pile I adored.

"You better not stand so close. It's moving this way. Where's all your family?" A man's voice said behind me.

I turned around but could hardly see through my tears.

"You were wonderful," he went on, "hauling that buggy away from your father's store."

"Oh, I'm so upset—and it looks as if it never would stop. I'm afraid our houses will catch next—"

Then the swirling crowd separated us and he was gone.

The great blaze kept up till midnight, spotting the dark night with sudden flashes of red, and spreading over the whole town an ominous halo of light. For a long time I watched its destruction. It seemed the end of the world.

The next morning, the heaviest gloom pervaded our breakfast table at my sister's house, Mrs. Andrew Haben's.

"Well, Mama," Papa said, "we're just about cleaned out. I think I can borrow enough to build a new store—and it'll be brick this time—two fires in one year are enough—but I don't know what I'll do to stock it. Or where we will live."

"You'll manage somehow, Papa. You always have."

When we went down street, everyone was already outside estimating the damage, throwing dirt over a few smouldering places, and pulling debris out of the wreckage to see if there were any salvage value. You cannot imagine the spirit of that town! Hardly anyone was talking about losses. But on all sides there was earnest talk of dimensions and materials, for these eager people were impatient to get to work on their new buildings. Many families had lost their homes and had bunked in with friends, sitting up most of the night to tell of exciting side adventures that had befallen them that frightful day. As we came by, many of them ran out to repeat these stories to us.

Papa and his partner, Mr. Cameron, set to work on their plans, too. Within the year they had erected at 21 Main Street, now numbered to be 64, a splendid brick and stone building which cost $4,000. Papa's interest in the store had to be very much less because practically all his capital (which was around $75,000) had gone in the fires. The bank really owned the store and Papa worked for a salary as a merchant tailor despite the fact that he had opened the third clothing store in Oshkosh and in the early days had been one of its most enterprising business men. I know this was very galling to Mama's pride but I was too young and heedless then to really understand how deep was her humiliation. My own affairs absorbed me.

"The belle of Oshkosh!"

That was my nickname—and more. So many times did I hear myself thus described that I had decided I really was the belle of Oshkosh. And because I had my three younger brothers, all near my own age, and their friends to associate with, it was only to be expected that I should gravitate toward the opposite sex. As I had grown older, Mama, who was very proud of my looks, encouraged me in this tendency.

By the time I was sixteen I was five feet four, as tall as I was ever to be. In later years it amused me very much the way in which writers all across the country would refer to me as "regal" or "queenly" considering how short I actually was. But I could understand how they came to choose those words because I always kept my carriage meticulously correct—no matter what hardships or disappointments, my chin was high—and that must have given an illusion of greater height. Perhaps I really did seem "queenly."

All my life people have complimented me on the sweet flash of my smile which gave them a glimpse of my even white teeth, and made my bright blue, far-apart Irish eyes sparkle merrily. I have never lost my smile. But at twenty I had a peaches-and-cream complexion, and a curving, rounded figure which everyone found very seductive. My hair was light golden, rather reddish, and naturally curly. My nose was slightly tip-tilted, and my mouth was rounded and soft. My ready wit was the true Irish "gift of gab."

Brought up in such an energetic town by industrious, ambitious parents, I was naturally very high-spirited. In addition, I had a marvelous constitution, which stood me in good stead all my life—I was seldom to have need of a doctor except when my babies were born. My parents and brothers spoiled me and men all around paid me attention. It was only natural that I should be headstrong, and feel no need for the friendship of women—especially since I could clearly see they were jealous.

All during the next months Oshkosh was hard at work with the same spirit it had shown the year before—as always immune to the heart-break of recurrent disaster. In 1875, the people built four hundred and seventy-six brick and fireproof buildings, and laid ten miles of sidewalk. That was a

12

herculean task for a town of seventeen thousand—but do it they did! By now, though, I was too busy with my beaux to pay much attention to anything except my flirtations. I was going to dances and sociables, attending the theatre, taking buggy rides behind smart trotters, and sailing with yachting parties on thirty-mile Lake Winnebago.

"You oughtn't to sit up until midnight sewing for that girl and making her clothes," Papa would complain to Mama. "And you ought to chaperone her more—she'll get a bad name."

But Mama would just laugh.

"Lizzie will take care of herself. She's got a head on her shoulders. I wouldn't be surprised if she became a great actress and why not, with her looks? Besides, I want her to have all the good times I missed!"

Papa would turn away with a shudder. He did not approve of Mama's encouraging me in my desire to go on the stage, or of her taking me to matinees whenever we had a little extra money to spend. He would put on his hat and leave quietly by the back door to pray alone in church. To him McCourt Hall had merely been a place to bring in rentals. He never watched the shows and he felt our souls inclined too much toward the paths of sin.

One April evening in 1876 my brother, Peter, and I took a walk. I stopped to get up on an enormous keg of nails to peer through a window into a new house where the men had stopped work. Behind me, I heard my brother, Pete, say:

"Hello!"

I turned around, and there was a very nice-looking young man standing on a lumber pile, also inspecting what the workmen had accomplished. All of us young people were very much interested in this particular house because the owners had sent all the way to Chicago for the latest wall-papers. As far as I could see, they were gold and brown flowered patterns, but the dining-room paper was still in rolls on the floor, and looked as if it were going to be a red geometric design.

"Hello," the young man said. "Is that your sister?"

"Yes," Pete answered proudly, "my sister Elizabeth."

"Hello," the stranger said to me shyly, "I'm Harvey Doe."

"Oh yes," I replied, "I know who you are. Your father comes into the store."

"Yes," he answered slowly—and then with a rush, "and he says you're the prettiest girl in town."

After blurting out this he blushed, stepped off the lumber pile, and started down the street.

"Well, I'll settle him—" Pete began menacingly.

"Oh, don't, Pete. I'm sure he didn't mean anything. Look how he blushed. I think he wanted to be nice."

Secretly, I was very pleased.

"Funny way of showing it," Pete grumbled. But with that the episode was closed and we both gave our thoughts to other youthful interests.

He had spoken in a soft, refined voice, and I was quite attracted. I arranged with my older brother, Jim, to bring him over to call a few nights later. I noticed how different he was from most of the chaps I knew. He seemed more quiet and chivalrous. When I had seen him on the street, I had thought his shyness just gawky, rather peculiar in a grown-up, but now it seemed strangely attractive. I began to look at him with fresh appreciation.

Harvey Doe stayed several hours, visiting with us all that evening, and from that night on I began to feel real affection.. Everything was more serious after that. Mama asked him to come to supper one night soon and he accepted. I had found my true love at last.

That winter there was more than usually good skating. Oshkosh was always famous for its ice and, before artificial refrigeration came in, at certain times of the winter the lake would be covered with a great band of men and troops of horses, cutting ice. Each team of horses drew an ice "plough" which had seven cast-steel cutters on it. Naturally, with the residential district sloping right down from a little elevation to this lake, everyone did lots of skating and had skating parties in the winter.

"Did you know the young men at our church are going to have a competition for the best skater on Saturday afternoon?" Harvey Doe said to me one evening. "I'm going to try for the first prize—though I don't suppose I shall have a chance."

Harvey's family belonged to the Methodist and Congregational Churches—in fact his uncle, the Reverend F. B. Doe, had preached the opening-day sermon when they finished building their church that year of 1875. He had also preached in Central City, Colorado, in the first years of the gold rush where he had gone to visit his brother, Harvey's father, who had mining interests in the famous camp. His family was the sort of Protestants who thought of Catholics almost as heathen idol-worshippers. Harvey never said anything to me about their attitude, but I had heard from the neighbors that his mother wasn't a bit pleased with his seeing so much of a "Romanist and Papist."

"I'd just like to show Mrs. Doe up," I thought to myself—I was an extraordinarily good skater, and could do all sorts of figures and arabesques—so I asked aloud:

"Who's going to be allowed to compete?"

"Oh, anyone in Oshkosh who wants to and can pay the entrance fee—it isn't really a church affair. It's just to make money for some of our church charities."

That settled the matter with me. All the next week I stole down to the lake and practiced in a secluded spot. I knew no other girl would enter, since it wasn't considered ladylike to appear in public lifting one's legs as it was necessary to do to be a good figure skater. But I didn't care about that—I would really rather enjoy shocking the town.

I kept my plan a secret from everyone except Mama. She thought it would be as much fun as I, and started fixing over a green woolen outfit I had. She shortened the skirt and trimmed a green hat with a band of fur to go with the dress. One of her dearest possessions was a set of mink—a long tippet and a muff to match. She loaned me these to wear, and I practiced two afternoons with them on. I had to get used to balancing and keeping in motion while still holding the muff gracefully.

Saturday afternoon arrived. Pretty nearly the whole town was gathered on the bank, sitting on rugs or grouped around little bonfires. The judges were three older men very important in the community—I think one of them was Mr. James Clark, the match manufacturer. I had just made my entry under the name of L. McCourt. Everyone thought it was one of my brothers, not paying much attention to the first initial. Imagine their consternation when my name was called and I stepped out from the crowd at the bank!

"Lizzie McCourt!"—I could hear my name being whispered all around from one group to another and I could also imagine the raised eyebrows of Mrs. Doe. It really amused me. I took several little running steps on my skates and then sailed out onto the ice and into the improvised rink. As I twirled and skimmed by the judge's stand, they smiled. I knew in my heart it was only the women on the banks who would be against me. The men had too ready a twinkle for the fetching figure I was cutting in my green and brown outfit.

It was great fun having all the eyes of the town focused on my movements and instead of being frightened I found the experience exhilarating. This is what it would be like if I ever got to be a great actress! My performance passed in a dream, and seemed over in a moment. Soon I was sitting on the bank again with Mama while she tucked me up under a laprobe from the buggy.

"You were wonderful, dear," she said, her eyes aglow with excitement.

The contest went on, but I was so thrilled with my daring that I couldn't concentrate on the other competitors. What was my surprise, though, a little later to hear one of the judges call out:

"First prize—Miss McCourt."

Me, the only girl among all those boys and men! I really was tickled to have won over them all. I scrambled out of the laprobe as fast as I could and hurried on to the ice to receive the blue ribbon and box of candy that was being held out to me. First prize, Miss McCourt!

Harvey came over after supper to call.

"You really were wonderful, Lizzie," he said. "Mother and I quarreled about you all the way home, but I think you were superb. I just knew I loved you when I saw you out there on the ice before all those people—not even perturbed—it was glorious—and I know now that I want to marry you."

"Why, Harvey . . ."

This was not the first proposal I had had, but it was the first to move me deeply.

Harvey had always seemed to me different from the other men of the town, and he was different. He would come over to play the piano for all my family in the evening, seeming to love us all. He would join in the general fun without trying to monopolize me, like most of the other men.

He wasn't so terribly much older than I, under two years, but he seemed older. He was always so considerate and unselfish. Though shy, he carried his years with a dignified air of responsibility. I think it was this, added to his

15

sweetness, and musical talent that made him stand out from the others. Anyway, deep down in my heart I must have known for a long time that I was just waiting for Harvey.

"But, Harvey, what will we live on? If your family doesn't approve of me, what can you do?"

"I think Father knows how I feel—he'll help us. He said something the other day about sending me out to to see about some mining property he's part owner of at Central City, Colorado. We'll go West and make our fortune overnight in gold. People are doing it all the time out there!"

Love and adventure all at once!

It seemed as if my whole life were blossoming into one great golden sunburst that evening. For some time I had been gazing across the broad waters of Lake Winnebago and picturing the world beyond. The more I thought about it, the more I knew I didn't want to settle down in Oshkosh. I wanted to try my wings—with Harvey! But I still didn't say anything to him as we sat there.

"Let's just be secretly engaged for a while," Harvey went on, "until you get used to the idea. And maybe Mother will change—."

Romance began for me then, warming gradually each day into a brighter and more glowing emotion. It was several months before I even told Mama what I was planning. I kept right on seeing other men meanwhile. But more and more I knew girls were saying catty things behind my back, insinuating I was fast. Several older women had cut me dead ever since the skating contest, and I was beginning to be not only restive, but rebellious.

"It'll certainly show them all up if I marry Harvey!" I said to Mama, with a toss of my head.

The Doe family was very much respected in Oshkosh. Harvey's father, W. H. Doe, was so important in the community that one of the new fire houses and steamers, located at 134 High Street was named after him—the W. H. Doe Steamer. The snobbish girls who said I was just the common daughter of an Irish tailor would certainly have to eat their words if I were Mrs. W. H. Doe, Jr.

"Pay no attention to them, Bessie," Mama said. "They're just jealous of your looks—and wish they could attract men as easily as you do."

But, little by little, they *were* bothering me, and more wholly and longingly I was falling in love with Harvey. He was very sympathetic with all my pet foibles, and was the only man I ever met who encouraged me to develop my acting ability. He said that naturally anyone as beautiful and talented as I had the right to be seen by many people. That would only be possible if I were on the stage.

"Only I love you and need you much more than audiences who haven't yet had a chance to know you!" he would add, with a beseeching, tremulous smile.

But I wanted more time and it was not until spring, 1877, that we actually announced our engagement. When we finally told our plans, the Does were very bitter. They said things about me, and even added to remarks made in the town —at least Mrs. Doe did. Mr. Doe did not feel that way, but he probably felt he couldn't contradict his wife and relatives.

Mama made a glorious trousseau and spent much more money than she should have, which made Papa either complain disagreeably, or brood in long sulky silences. I kept telling him Harvey and I would make such a splendid fortune in Colorado that in no time I could pay him back. But Papa was getting old, and this didn't cheer him up a bit. My younger brothers and sister, however, especially Claudia, were thrilled at the prospect of picking gold nuggets off the ground or from the creek beds! Their eyes would get as big as silver dollars while I talked to them of the marvelous life Harvey and I were going to lead out West.

I had always thought the morning of my wedding day would be the happiest of my life, but somehow this wasn't. I couldn't tell why. As I jumped out of bed and ran to the window to see what the day was like I had a brief feeling of foreboding. Quickly I shook it off and made myself think:

"Ridiculous! You're worried because Mrs. Doe has been so difficult and at the last minute may not come to the wedding at all—or make a scene in front of all the guests."

Soon my chin was up, and I was light-hearted and gay again, planning ahead for the golden future that was to be Harvey's and mine—dreaming those fairy-tale dreams of a happy bride who is setting out on the hopeful path of marriage with the man she loves devotedly.

The rest of that day, June 27, 1877, went smoothly enough. I was twenty-two and Harvey was twenty-three. We were married by Father James O'Malley at St. Peter's Church. My brother-in-law, Andrew Haben, was mayor of Oshkosh that year and both our families were so well-known that crowds were standing in the street and the church was overflowing. We had a small reception afterward. Mrs. Doe was cold and taciturn and repressed, but at least she was not openly rude to me or any of my family. Mr. Doe was obviously happy, but whether because of our marriage or because Harvey was going to Central City to carry on with his mining interests I couldn't tell.

Harvey's shy eyes were alight and full of ecstatic unbelief every time I looked at him. Mama was pleased and exuberant, playing the benevolent hostess. I was triumphant, young and extravagantly hopeful. It was thus I became Mrs. William H. Doe, Jr.

As we left to go to the station I took a last, reflective look at Oshkosh, "The Sawdust City." Factories and mills burst with the rattle and clang of industry. Across the two wagon bridges of the city moved streams of traffic. Here in the bustle and excitement of a frontier town I had been cradled. But now it was frontier no longer—and I was eager to follow that exciting horizon Westward. Although I was sorry to leave my family and home, I was breathless to be off.

"Darling, now our life is really beginning," Harvey whispered to me as we stood on the little open back platform of the train pulling away from the station.

I leaned against him for support, and thrilled to the thought. We waved handkerchiefs to our family and friends as long as we could see them, shaking the rice from our clothes at the same time. Finally, laughing merrily when Oshkosh was no more than a blur in the distance, we turned into the train and took our seats in the coach.

Outside the rolling, hilly country of Wisconsin was abloom. Green grassy fields and waving marshes were flying past—or at least we thought of our speed as flying. The little train really made not much more than fifteen miles an hour, I imagine. But it seemed to me, who had never ridden on a train before, that we were literally hurtling through space.

"I love you, my sweet, beautiful little bride!" Harvey whispered passionately, pressing my hand and looking adoringly into my eyes. His words were like a song, sung to the rhythm and bounce of wheels along the tracks—an urgent, earthy obligato.

"And I love you, darling Harvey."

Our honeymoon had begun—the world was fair, and all life lay before us— I couldn't possibly describe the intoxication of that moment!

After an arduous trip, steaming endlessly, it seemed, across prairie lands of the Great American Desert, we arrived in Colorado. My first glimpse of the Rockies, viewed from the train window one morning, did something to me I was never to get over. All the adjectives in the language have been used to describe that sight, by explorers, by learned travelers, by writers, and by humble people keeping diaries. And still it was an experience so important in my own life that I, too, must try.

People have said they "rise up" suddenly—and so they do. But to me, on that bright, crisp morning, they seemed to have been let down from the sky, like a gigantic backdrop on the stage of the world, their colors of grey and red and startling white painted on by a Master Hand. They looked unreal, like an experience from another world, but at the same time an experience of such magnitude and importance that I must bow in worship before their granite strength and snow-white purity.

"Aren't they gorgeous?" Harvey asked.

"They're more than gorgeous," I answered reverently, then silently prayed to their rugged magnificence that, to the end, the power the sight of them gave me might never wane.

Some premonition told me in that moment my prayer would be heeded. I could not suspect what those mountains would do in the shaping of my life, but I was sure they would shape it. And so they did. I was never again to be away from their influence, and only for brief periods away from their sight. I loved them instinctively that day—and I never lost that love—strange though it may seem for a girl brought up beside the water.

"They are our future" I added to Harvey, my voice trembling with excitement.

"Yes!"

My future, yes—but not our future. Still, I could not know that, then, nor even guess it. But deep in my bones, I felt their power.

Denver in those days was a turbulent, thriving community, the trading and outfitting center of all the dramatic mining activities of the state. It had grown into a town of over thirty thousand population. Pioneers struck it rich in the hills, but they brought their wealth to Denver to spend.

And spend it they did! I had never been in a hotel like the American House. Every sort of cosmopolitan figure dotted its elegant lobby, carpeted in red. These glamorous people smiled at me and invited my husband into the bar. Five years before, the Grand Duke Alexis had been entertained in the sumptuous dining-room of the hotel, transformed for the occasion into a ballroom, and the hosts were all the great names of Colorado. The belles of Central City (where I was now bound) had come down from the mountains by stagecoach for the event. This was high adventure, colorful pageantry—and I was a part of it. This was a new world, where European royalty and English nobility moved perfectly naturally. Those dreams I had dreamed on the shores of Lake Winnebago, at home in Oshkosh, were actually coming true.

Meanwhile, during our fortnight's honeymoon, Harvey was studying miners' tools and equipment in the stores of Larimer Street and getting ready to meet his father in Blackhawk for the mile's drive to Central City. When we started for Colorado's great gold camps, I was tremendously stirred and elated. I had been listening avidly to the many tales of untold fortunes already made from the district's famous "blossom rock." I was sure that ours was the next treasure tale that would come out of Central City to be told over the massive bars of Larimer Street—the story of how clever Harvey Doe had presented his beautiful bride with a gold mine that would make her a millionaire only a few months after they were married!

The train that bore us westward toward James Peak puffed along in a steep canon beside the gushing waters of Clear Creek, a creek no longer clear, but green-grey in color because of the tailings from the new-fangled mills that had been introduced to treat the ore. I was disappointed in the looks of that water and I wondered if there were to be other disappointments for me ahead, in those great mountains. But I put the thought aside and went back to the vision of myself as an elegant social leader in Denver—

How soon would these mountains answer my prayers—or would they answer at all?

Chapter Two

The miners in the Central City district were changing shifts at noon. In the midst of the turmoil Harvey and I got off the train at Blackhawk and caught the stage for the mile's ride up Gregory Gulch after being handed a note from Mr. Doe directing us to a boarding house where rooms were awaiting. As the miners scuffed along the dusty road in their heavy boots, swinging lunch pails, they drifted into groups. From nearly every one of these burst song, each group lending an air to the intermingled medley. I was able to follow some of the melodies, which were of such a haunting quality I leaned forward and tapped the driver on the back.

"What are those men singing?" I asked.

"Cornish songs. The miners are all Cousin Jacks hereabouts—that is, that ain't Irish. That's why you see so much good stonework in them retaining walls and buildings around here. When we git into Central, look up at our school 'n 'Piscopal Church. Built by Cornishmen, or Cousin Jacks, as we calls 'em. They brought the knack from the old country."

"But how do they have such splendid voices?"

"Oh, them's natural. Real musical people—and then all the high-class people gets them into singin' societies and sech. Last March a group put on "The Bohemian Girl" and now we're goin' to build the only Opry House in Colorado for jest sech goin's-on. When we don't have shows goin' through, we have some sort of doin's of our own. We're the up-and-comin'est camp in the West. Got some hankerin' for higher things."

I looked about me again after I heard this. It sounded odd to me that a mining camp should be interested in culture but it also seemed encouraging. I was thrilled to think they were building an opera house and that the town specialized in amateur theatricals. I felt certain I had come to the right place. Besides winning love and riches in this strange setting, I would also get my long-cherished wish to go on the stage!

The setting was certainly strange enough to my eyes accustomed, as I was, to flat, rolling country. The towns of Blackhawk, Mountain City, Central City, Dogtown, and Nevadaville were all huddled on top of each other in the narrow bottom of stark, treeless gulches in the most puzzling jigsaw fashion, but totaling nearly 6,000 people. Mines, ore dumps, mills, shafthouses, blacksmith shops, livery stables, railroad trestles, cottages and fine residences were perched at crazy angles, some on stilts, and scrambled together with no semblance of order while they emitted an assortment of screeching, throbbing and pounding noises.

The only corner that had any form at all was the junction of Lawrence St., Main St. and Eureka St. in the business section of Central City. Lawrence and Eureka were really continuations of the same street but Main came uphill at a funny slant from where Spring and Nevada Gulches met so that on one corner, a saloon, the building had to be shaped like a slice of pie and across from it, the First National Bank building had a corner considerably wider than a right angle.

The air of the business buildings, despite their odd architectural lines, was very substantial since, as the driver explained, they had all been rebuilt in brick and stone just three years before, after Central had had two disastrous fires in 1873 and 1874. I knew the tragedy of fire in pioneer communities and sighed, remembering how Papa had lost his money. This part of Central was more prepossessing than what we had driven through. The rest was too battered from eighteen years' careless usage in men's frenzy to tear the gold from the many lodes that crossed Gregory Gulch—the Bobtail, Gregory, Bates and other famous producers.

The driver pointed out our boarding house on the other side of town up Roworth St., behind where the railway station would be when they completed the switchback track that they were now building to climb the 500 feet rise from Blackhawk to Central. Harvey and I started to gather up our valises and carryalls. We told the express office to hold our trunk until we knew our plans more definitely and trudged off. We met Colonel Doe coming down the hill to meet us.

"Hello, there, you newlyweds," he called. "I'm sorry I couldn't meet you at Blackhawk but I can't drive our buggy in these hills until I get a brake put on it."

Colonel Doe had a tall, commanding presence and he looked particularly well against this mammoth country. He was always very bluff and genial and he seemed to suit these boisterous, breezy surroundings. He laughed now at the joke on himself.

"I thought I was being so smart to ship our two-seated buggy out here to save money. But the blasted thing's no danged good without a brake! After we have dinner, which is all ready at the boarding house, we'll drive to a blacksmith shop and get it fixed up. Then we'll go see the mine."

So that's what we did. We drove to the blacksmith shop of John R. Morgan, a Welshman who told my father-in-law he had settled in Wisconsin when he first came over from Wales. Later he had moved farther West. In turn, Colonel Doe told Morgan how he had lived in Central the first years of its existence and how after selling out, had gone back to Wisconsin where he was in the legislature in 1866 and had lived there ever since. While the buggy was being outfitted, the older men had a pleasant time exchanging comparisons of the two places.

Harvey and I, meanwhile, talked to Mr. Morgan's son, Evan. He was a handsome nineteen-year-old lad who helped around the shop, shoeing heavy ore teams while his father completed more complicated iron-work commissions. He was quite stocky and strong and later did our work for the mine, shoeing horses and making ore buckets. Their shop was on Spring Street, just a stone's throw from the Chinese alley whose joss sticks had started Central's worst conflagration. He was very affable, had a good Welsh voice and sang me a few Celtic airs when I spoke of the Cornishmen I had heard singing earlier.

After the buggy was equipped for mountain travel, we set off for our mine. I could hardly wait I was so excited. We bumped and scratched along up the stiff pull of Nevada Street to Dogtown, turning out frequently to let four-horse ore wagons pass, and then we tacked back along Quartz Hill to the shafthouse. And there it was—the Fourth of July mine!

I'll never forget how elated and excited I was, inspecting the mine that day, little knowing what sorrow it was to bring. The mine was half Colonel Doe's and half Benoni C. Waterman's. They had bought it in 1871 but very little work had been done on it. Father Doe's idea was to lease the Waterman half on a two-year agreement and sink the shaft 200 feet deeper, timbering it well. Then if the Fourth of July opened up the ore he expected, Harvey could buy out the Waterman interest for $10,000 the first year or $15,000 the second. If the ore didn't materialize after the two years were up, then Waterman was free to sell his one-half interest anytime he wanted. Colonel Doe would give all profits on his share to Harvey and if he made good, would deed it outright to us in a year.

Everything sounded glorious to me. I clapped my hands and hugged my bulky father-in-law in appreciation.

"Oh, you're just too wonderful!" I cried. "I know your gift is going to make Harvey and me rich. Then I can help poor Mama and Papa out of all their troubles in bringing up such a large family. You're a dear."

The summer eased smoothly along. Harvey and I rented a little cottage on Spring Street to live in and while I was busy getting settled, I began to learn the spell of Colorado's gaunt, tremendous mountains. By the middle of August, the lawyers had completed the agreement between Father Doe and Mr. Waterman and we had waved our benefactor off home to Oshkosh from the station at Blackhawk. I wanted Harvey to record the agreement immediately as a crew was already working at the mine. But after Father Doe left, I began to find out what Harvey was really like—his shyness was just weakness. He was lazy and procrastinating and he thought because he was a Doe that everything should be done for him.

He was not as big as his father in height or in character. Father Doe had lived in Central with his wife during the Civil War years and owned a large parcel of mining claims in both Nevadaville and Central City, a mill and a large residence in Prosser Gulch, and a boarding house nearby for the miners. He invested $5,000 and made so much profit, particularly from the Gunnell and Wood mines in Prosser Gulch, up at the head of Eureka Street, that he was able to retire rich in June, 1865, after the War was over. He made a trip to New York and closed with the Sierra Madre Investment Co., taking payment partly in cash and partly in ownership with the company. After that, he returned home to Oshkosh and occupied himself with lumber lands in Wisconsin. But he made occasional trips back to Central as superintendent of the Sierra Madre Co. He was a good business man and very civic in his interests.

But not so with his son. Three weeks later, I, myself, had to fetch out the buggy, hitch up the team, and drive Harvey to the Court House to have the agreement recorded. That day was September 6, 1877, and I remember what a peculiar sensation it gave me watching Harvey write his legal name, W. H. Doe, Jr. He and his signature seemed suddenly just a tenuous shadow of his father, a shadow having no existence if the body that casts it, moves away.

"Oh, this isn't like me!" I thought, shaking my curls in disapproval of my doubt. "I'm really very confident—not morbid. I just *know* Colorado will be good to me."

We stepped out again into the September briskness and I urged him to hurry with sinking and timbering the shaft as per agreement.

"You want to get a lot of work done before the snow flies," I urged.

He seemed wavering but I handed him the reins and urged him on toward the mine.

"I'm sure everything will be all right, dear," I added.

At the bottom of the street we kissed and I stood there watching my young husband as he drove off up the road toward Nevadaville. All around were crowds of men intent on their business, driving heavy ore-wagons whose teams lurched with the weight and whose brakes screeched on the steep grades. Others were loading ore cars with waste and dumping them off the end of little tracks laid out on high hillocks jutting precariously into the blue sky. The steady rhythm of pumps and the whir of steam hoists resounded from each hill. You could even hear the narrow gauge railroad whistle at Blackhawk shrieking its demoniac energy while bringing in machinery, huge and unwieldy, for the hoists of mine shafts, for the stamp mills crunching ore, and a hundred other purposes. Near its track at many points were sluice boxes carrying water back to the creek after being denuded of its placer wealth. Everywhere were serious men busy making money. Gold was king!

The main street was crowded with women going to market on foot, carpet bags or carry-alls slung on their arm for supplies, some of them leading burros to pack their purchases. Most of the bars were open and men, off work at the mines, idled in and out or lounged briefly in the strangely bright Colorado sunshine of this mild day. Others were to be seen on doorsteps, chewing tobacco, chatting or whittling on an old wheel spoke. The banks were open for business and cashiers from the mines were taking in gold dust, nuggets and retorts to be weighed. It did not seem possible that among all this hustle and industry there would be no place for us.

"Hello, there, Baby! Want a ride?"

I raised my eyes. Two dashing young men, quite well dressed, expensive Stetsons on their heads, were in a gig that trotted past. They looked like mining engineers or mill managers. I couldn't help smiling at their handsome, good-humored appearance, and one of them swept off his Stetson and bowed low. The other, with the reins, pulled up the horse.

"You're much too pretty and young to be standing alone on a street corner," he said.

"And you're too fresh! I've just been seeing my husband off to his mine, thank you," I replied as I flounced around and started up the hill with a great show of indignation and temper. Actually, I was quite flattered.

"When did you come to camp?" he called, paying no attention to my attitude and slapping his horse with the reins to follow along beside me on the board walk.

I did not reply but kept on climbing steadily as fast as I could go up Spring Street, puffing for wind in the high altitude.

"Oh, leave her alone, Slim—she's a nice girl. Come on, I want to get down to the post office."

"Hell, all right. Well, good-bye, Baby—you better tell your husband to watch out or big bad men will be after you."

I was really furious now. I could see he didn't believe I was a married woman. He took me for just a common girl of the streets. Turning around, I stamped my foot and started to yell at him when the other one said:

"No offense, ma'am. Slim, here, hasn't seen a girl like you in so long he's forgotten his manners."

They wheeled their horse and started off down toward Main Street, leaving me still gasping on the walk. I had been insulted. I wanted to cry, to cry for the shame of it! But as their trim backs receded in the swift-wheeling gig, I told myself this was what I had come for—adventure. And here it was. I ended by trudging on up hill with a smile flickering at the corners of my mouth.

But the smile was not to remain long. When Harvey returned that night he was dirty and tired and discouraged. He had taken a lot of samples from

23

the sump of the shaft to the assay office. But a man he had gone to for advice in Nevadaville hadn't thought the samples worth bothering to pay for assaying.

"You might keep on sinking your shaft and strike a better vein. But these quartz lodes you got down there now are too low grade to work," had been his verdict.

What to do now? My heart flew into my throat. We had had only the money that Harvey's father had left us to get started on. In a few more weeks with running a crew at the mine, our capital would be used up and if the ore were no good, we would have nothing to live on. But if we did try to keep on we might strike high-grade ten feet beyond—just like so many bonanza kings. That's what I wanted to do and suggested we borrow money at the bank.

"I'll help you, Harvey, I'm strong."

Our little house on Spring Street was not very well tended because for six months, besides being wife and housekeeper, I donned miner's clothes to run the horse-pulled hoist in our mine. We each worked a crew on separate shafts. For several months we had rich ore, then the vein went "in cap." We kept on sinking, but all to no avail. We still didn't strike high-grade ore and the shaft caved from faulty timbering.

"I guess I better get a job in one of the big mines," Harvey suggested.

Me, the wife of a common miner—working for a few dollars a day! The idea struck horror to my soul.

"Certainly not!" I replied. "I won't have it."

"Well, what else is there to do? We can't go home. Father would be mad and Mother won't have you in the house."

"Your mother—with her airs. I'm just as good as she is any day!"

"I'll thank you not to insult my mother."

Words tumbled on words like blows. Harvey and I were in the midst of our first serious quarrel. The higher our tempers rose, the more bitter our choice of barbs to hurt each other. I hated the idea of having married a man who would give up. I thought I had married a clever man. Instead, I had married a weakling. I said all this and more.

"I've been brought up by self-respecting people who only spend what they've got," Harvey replied heatedly. "We haven't got the money to fulfill the agreement of timbering in a "good, substantial, workmanlike manner"—and besides, it's too long a gamble. I don't know enough about carpentry and mining. It's better for me to learn what I'm about first by taking a steady job. Then, when I know more, and maybe have saved up some money of our own, we can try developing the mine."

I thought this plan was cowardly and stupid. Maybe development would be a long gamble, but all mining was a gamble—even life was a gamble—and only those who had the courage to play could win.

But not Harvey Doe. He got a job mucking in the Bobtail Tunnel. We gave up our little house on Spring St. and moved down to Blackhawk, the milling and smelting center, partly to be close to the Bobtail and partly because Blackhawk being less good socially, was cheaper. We lived in two rooms of a red brick building on Gregory Street (which today has Philip Rohling painted on the door). The building was close to one erected by Sandelowsky, Pelton & Co., prosperous dry goods and clothing merchants of Central, who decided to open a branch store in Blackhawk in 1878. They occupied the corner space on the station end of Gregory Street. In our building, a store was on each side of the center stairs and living rooms occupied the second floor. I was hardly more than a bride—yet look to what I had descended!

One bright ray of hope remained—and I tried to keep thinking of it. Since I was sure after Harvey's inefficiency, Father Doe would never deed us over his share of the Fourth of July, I had persuaded Harvey to buy some claims. I still clung to my dream of riches from out of the earth and when the Does had sent us $250 at Christmas, in January, 1878, we spent $50 for a claim on the Stonewall Lode in Prosser Gulch and $165 for three lodes on Quartz Hill not far from the Fourth of July and adjoining the English-Kansas mine. These were the Troy, Troy No. 2 and Muscatine Lodes. I had great belief in that property—fortunes were being made everyday from Quartz Hill—and if we could just develop our mine, we would, too!

Loneliness and poverty was my lot in the meantime. I had no friends and I used to take walks around Blackhawk to amuse myself. There was a Cousin Jennie, a Mrs. Richards, who liked to garden and occasionally I would go to see her. She would always pick me a bouquet of flowers for our room because she said I was so beautiful that posies suited me.

"You are like a seraph—an angel!" I can remember her saying.

To help while away the time I began a scrap-book. Things that interested me I would cut out and paste in its leaves. Left alone so much, I turned to my day-dreaming more and more, and watched for poetry, cartoons and other informative subjects to put in my book. I also read the fashion magazines and clipped pictures from them, especially members of royalty and society figures dressed up—I don't know why, since it looked as if I was never again to have enough money for pretty, chic clothes.

"Everything is so different from what I expected," was the thought that kept running through my unhappy mind.

Although Harvey and I were living in such close quarters, we seemed to grow further away from each other. When he was on a shift that went to work at seven in the morning he would come home in the afternoon so tired, being unused to hard work, that all he would do in the evening was read a book or write home. He spent hours composing long letters to his mother. I resented these letters very much, but I tried not to say anything while awaiting the day when he had saved enough money to start development again.

Later, he was on a shift that went to work at night and I hardly saw him. He would come home long after I had gone to bed. Meanwhile, I had nothing to occupy my time, as I did not especially like any of the women in the rooming house. For amusement, I would make long visits, looking at the bolts of cloth and other wares in Sandelowsky-Pelton, the store on our street. That's how I came to know Jacob Sandelowsky who had been with the firm since 1866. When I met him, he was a bachelor, medium tall and twenty-six years old. Whenever he was in the Blackhawk store, he paid me extravagant compliments and we would talk about the clothing business as I had learned it from Papa's experience with McCourt and Cameron, later Cameron and McCourt, as Papa became poorer. Occasionally, he made me gifts, particularly dainty shoes which he brought down from the Central City store.

Then Harvey lost his job at the Bobtail. I don't know why. But I had already learned how unreliable he was and I suppose his bosses did, too. Because he had been the only boy in the family to grow up, his mother and four sisters spoiled him to such a degree that he was never able to succeed at anything. Soon he was becoming a drifter, drifting from one job to another and later from one camp to another, the women of the family helping him out if he was too close to starving. But they weren't helping him now because of their dislike of me—and we were very hungry!

I not only had the natural appetite of a healthy young woman but, as I had found I was going to have a baby, I craved additional food for the new life. At first, the news of my condition seemed to make things better. I wrote to Father Doe and he replied that his lumber mill had just burned down in Oshkosh. He would wind up his affairs in Oshkosh and move the family to Central. He wanted to be near his grandchild and he would straighten out Harvey's affairs.

Harvey's affairs certainly were tangled although he kept the whole truth from his father and from me for a long time. It turned out that besides the money he owed the First National Bank, a sum that later, with accumulating interest, amounted to over a thousand dollars, he had also secretly been employing a Peter Richardson to repair the badly timbered shaft of the Fourth of July that Harvey had botched. Peter Richardson had never been paid for his work nor for a new hoist he had installed and in May, 1878, obtained a judgment against Harvey for $485 plus court costs. The Newell Brothers also had a $48 bill against him for grain and hay for our team, run up before we had had to sell the horses. He was afraid to say anything about these bills to his father.

I was becoming desperate. My own family were too poor to appeal to and I was far too proud to want anyone in Oshkosh except Father Doe to guess at the truth of how my marriage had turned out. I turned more and more to Jake for comfort and every kind of sustenance.

Harvey began to spend his time in bars, not that he drank much, just a few beers. But hanging around and talking to the customers gave him ample opportunity to feel sorry for himself and to tell people his troubles. I hated him for his weakness—I always detested any kind of blubbering. Soon we were quarreling regularly.

Although he got a few odd jobs and sometimes earned enough money for food, it was never enough to pay our rent and we were forced to move about a lot in Blackhawk and Central. That year and the next were two of the most discouraging I ever spent. I was constantly blue and dejected in spirit and frightened for the future of my baby. To try to help out, I put on miner's clothes and attempted to do some work starting to sink a shaft on the Troy Lode next to the English-Kansas that Harvey had bought from the Hinds brothers. I really was in no condition to do this work but I knew that many of the mines on

Quartz Hill, very close by, were steady lucrative producers and our claim seemed the one hope.

"Hello, there!" I heard one day, called out from a teamster driving an ore wagon down from the Patch mines up above. "What do you think you're doing? You're Baby Doe, aren't you?"

That's how I met Lincoln Allebaugh, "Link" as he was always called. He was a slim, fine-boned fifteen year old boy who, despite his age and small frame, could drive an ore wagon because of his knack with horses and excellent driving hands. He sometimes had trouble setting the brake and, after we knew him better, he would get Harvey to go along and apply his stocky strength. Link had been born in Blackhawk and lived there all his life. He knew who I was from seeing me in Jake's store and hearing Harvey call me by one of my family nicknames—Baby, which was also the one the miners in camp had spontaneously adopted.

"You're too little to do heavy work like that," Link said. "You better let me give you a lift home."

I felt the truth of what he had said in my bones. Suddenly, I was very tired, a new feeling for me and not a sensation I liked. While Link loaded my pick and shovel in with the ore, I climbed up on the high front seat.

From that day, one calamity followed another. My only friend was Jake and soon Harvey and I were quarreling about him, too. The year before in March, when Harvey had been working night shift, Jake had wanted to take me to the opening of the Opera House. The amateur players staged a gala two nights, putting on a concert the first night and two plays, "School" and "Cool as a Cucumber," on the second. Special trains had been run from Denver and the cream of society of the two most important towns in Colorado, Denver and Central, had attended, their festive gowns being reported in the *Rocky Mt. News* and the *Central City Register* the next day. It had been a thrilling occasion.

But Harvey had been indignant when I had suggested that I might go with Jake.

"No respectable married woman would think of doing a thing like that!" he had said hotly.

So I had watched the event, longingly, standing on a boardwalk across the street and yearning to be one of the gay throng, to be wearing a beautiful evening dress or even better, to be one of the amateur actresses from Central City playing on the stage. But I had been a good wife and obeyed Harvey— I had not gone.

Now it was different and I was defiant. Harvey could not support me and Jake had given us too many groceries and presents of merchandise not to admit the friendship openly.

"I'd be dead—starved to death—if it wasn't for Jake. He's helped us out over and over again when you didn't have a dime. I *won't* let you say things against him!"

Harvey was surly but said nothing more and soon took his bad temper out to dramatize in a saloon. But the next quarrel was the end. He insinuated that my baby wasn't his and I picked up a specimen of Fourth of July ore that we kept on the table and threw it at him with all the strength I could muster. The rock hit him on the neck, scratching him badly, and, as he felt the injured spot and the trickle of blood, he blurted out,

"Why, you common Irish hussy!"

He glared at me briefly, turned in awkward anger and stamped out the door. I did not see him again for months. I heard later that he had hitched a ride on a freight train out of camp.

When I told Jake what had happened, he said,

"Never mind, Baby, I'll see you through—and what you need now is some gayety to forget about your troubles. Let's go to the Shoo-Fly tonight."

The suggestion shocked me and I peered at my friend suspiciously but he only shrugged his shoulders and asked laconically:

"What difference does it make?"

I could see his point. If I went to the Shoo-Fly who was to know or care? My husband didn't value me enough to stay and protect me and he had been the first to unjustly impugn my good name.

The Shoo-Fly was Central's one flashy variety hall. It was in a brick building on Nevada St. (and still stands, beside a dignified residence shaded by a fine tall spruce tree in its front yard). It housed a reception room, bar, a dance hall, and a stage. Several private rooms for gambling and bedrooms were toward the back. Its entrance was off the street, up a long flight of wooden steps hung on the side of the building. These steps led to the rear of the second floor and into the reception room. There was also another entrance down from Pine Street, darker and less conspicuous.

The whole lay-out emphasized discretion but was the crimson spot of the town, dedicated to the flattery of weakness. Unattached men, of whom there were a great many in the camp, liked to come to this favorite rendezvous of sensational women. No nice, married lady would be seen there. But, so far, had any matron of gentility extended me the slightest kindness? If I met any in the streets they regarded me with a distrustful air, and passed on. It was their men who wanted to meet me.

"All right!" I determined. "I'll go."

I was terribly depressed and perhaps Jake was right that I needed cheering up. That night I put on my prettiest blue and pink foulard for it brought out the unusual blue of my eyes and the soft, fresh tints of my hair and cheeks. Together, we sallied forth.

When we turned off Main Street toward the Shoo-Fly stairs, I had one moment of panic as if I were taking an inevitable step, a step from which there would be no return, something like Caesar crossing the Rubicon. But I laughed the moment away—I was twenty-four years old, pretty and gay, and my friends said I had Irish wit. Surely life should give me more than a drab boarding house and the charity of one Jewish friend? I tossed my curls and stepped on.

Once inside, Jake ordered champagne. He enjoyed watching the dancing girls in the variety show and indulging in a little gambling. Later he brought several well-known men to join us at our table. It was fun to be laughing and talking with several new acquaintances.

"So you're Baby Doe!" one of the merry men with bold eyes reflected.

"I hear the manager of my mill tried to pick you up in the street one day, and you snubbed him!" He laughed as though greatly amused.

"I am Mrs. Harvey Doe, if you please. My husband is out of town on business."

"Well, you're Baby Doe to all the miners in camp! They all know you—your beauty's enough to advertise you, even if you didn't spend so danged much time walking all over the place. They've also told me how unfriendly you are."

"I'm not unfriendly. I'm delighted to meet people if they are properly introduced—"

"What are you doing here then? This is no place for a nice girl."

"I know it. But I'm so lonely that my good friend, Mr. Sandelowsky, offered to watch out for me if I came."

Baby Doe I was from that night on—and nearly every night I was at the Shoo-Fly under Jake's protection. It was lively and gay and I made lots of friends among the men and girls who frequented the place. As I got to know these sporting girls, I liked them much better than the girls I had known in Oshkosh. They weren't very well educated, but they had a great zest for living. Their generosity was genuine—their courage tremendous. None of the girls at home possessed such qualities. I really felt I understood them and when they seemed to like me, I knew they really did. That meant a great deal to a lonely girl.

"Why don't you get rid of that mama's-boy husband of yours? Why, with your looks, you could get any man you wanted!" one of them said to me.

Most of the talk at the Shoo-Fly that summer and autumn was about the sensational rise of silver and Leadville and Horace Tabor. It was like a fairy tale. For years, placer miners at the head of the Arkansas River had been irritated by peculiar black sand which was very heavy and could not be separated from the gold easily. A decade passed without their recognizing its true worth but during the '70s several miners worked on secret assays which proved the sand was eroding from carbonates of lead and silver ore. Quietly they began to look for veins and by 1877, after several mines had been located, the news was out.

A mad rush was on and many an odd fluke of luck followed. The veins did not outcrop on the surface. This made it possible for a prospector to start sinking a shaft almost anywhere and hit an ore body from a few feet to three hundred and fifty feet beneath the surface. That fact created some fantastic and astonishing fortunes.

Living in this locality for a number of years had been Horace Tabor, a middle-aged storekeeper. He and his wife were New Englanders who had come West in the first wild gold rush of '59 and after failing to make any money out of mining despite repeated attempts, had dismissed the gold bug from their heads. They had settled down with their one son, Maxcy, now grown, to a steady respectable middle-class life at Oro City, three miles from the site of what was later to be Leadville.

But silver was to change all that. During July, 1877, Tabor recognized the excitement in the air and moved his grocery stock and supplies from Oro City to a fairly large log cabin in Leadville. By January, 1878, about seventy cabins,

29

shanties and tents made up the camp and during the next month the inhabitants held a town election in which the forty-seven-year-old Tabor was chosen mayor. During the next few months the town grew and prospered and so did Tabor's store profits.

One spring day, two German prospectors, August Rische and George Hook, dropped into the grocery and asked Tabor if he would put up supplies for them to search for a vein of carbonates. Tabor had grubstaked many a miner to no avail but he was naturally generous. He probably expected no better this time, but he made an outlay of some seventeen dollars in return for an agreement that he was to have a third interest in any mine they found. Off they went and located a claim on Fryer Hill which they named the Little Pittsburgh.

They worked along steadily for some time and when their shaft was but twenty-six feet deep, they broke through the layer of hard rock they had been drilling into a body of soft, black, heavy ore. The next day, a fine May morning, Tabor left the grocery store in charge of Augusta, his efficient, managerial wife, and with pick and shovel wielded in vigorous, high anticipation, helped his partners dig and hoist the first wagon load of ore. The smelter bought it immediately for over $200!

By July nearly a hundred tons of ore were being hoisted and shipped each week and the three partners had an income of about fifty thousand dollars a month. Toward fall, Hook sold out to Tabor and Rische for $98,000 and Rische later sold out his interest plus some adjoining claims to Jerome B. Chaffee and David Moffat for over a quarter of a million dollars. Tabor clung to his share and the talk now was how he and his new partners had consolidated all their claims on Fryer Hill and incorporated for twenty million dollars. The fabulous story of silver and Leadville and Tabor—you heard it every night!

Everybody at the Shoo-Fly said Central was dying. Prof. N. P. Hill had taken his family to Denver and moved his smelter from Blackhawk to Argo, outside Denver. They quoted his opinion that no new strikes would be made in the district although the established producers might maintain their output for decades. In any case it would be cheaper hauling ore downhill to the smelter than coal up. Other top families were deserting the district. The Frank Halls, J. O. Raynolds and Eben Smiths had already gone and it was said that the George Randolphs, Henry Haningtons, Frank Youngs, Joseph Thatchers and Hal Sayres were contemplating departure. This kind of conversation was very depressing for me in addition to all my other troubles.

After that, things happened fast. I don't know what would have become of me if it hadn't been for Jake.

My baby boy came July 13, 1879, and was still-born. It was Jake who paid the bills and made all the arrangements. He was a marvelous friend. By then he was talking about opening a store in Leadville, and he told me he thought that was where I should go, too, that is, if I no longer loved Harvey. Rich strikes were being made there every day.

"Looks to me like he's deserted you. You have your own future to look out for now. First, see if you like it over there. Then, if you do, you can get a divorce for non-support and you'll be free to build a new life for yourself. Anyway, let me give you the trip and then decide."

My love for Harvey *was* dead, but I hated to think of the disgrace of divorce. That ignominy would kill Papa and Mama!

I had hoped that when Father Doe reached Central, matters would straighten out. The family moved just at the time that alone and destitute, I was having the humiliating, heart-rending experience of giving birth to a dead baby, attended only by a negro mid-wife. If the baby had lived, maybe my story would have been entirely different; but without that bond, I could not live down the calumnies that Mrs. Doe believed.

Father Doe opened a mining office in Central in 1879 and Harvey turned up again from wherever he had been to live with his parents. I suspected that he had spent the time in Oshkosh since Mrs. Doe proved more bitter about me than she had been before we were married, probably influenced by Harvey's lies. Father Doe came to see me several times and gave me money. He liked and felt sorry for me and tried to offset the contention of his wife that I had disgraced the Doe name.

I thought it was Harvey who had disgraced the Doe name by deserting me when I was pregnant; but for everyone's sake, that autumn of 1879, Harvey and I patched up our quarrel and tried to make a go of it again. A few months later, I thought I saw him go into a bagnio and I immediately ran across the street to demand: "Who's disgracing the Doe name now?" He said he was just collecting a bill . . . that he would never be unfaithful . . . But I wasn't sure . . .

The elder Does decided to move to Idaho Springs, inasmuch as Central was declining and there seemed to be no way of straightening out Harvey. For the next five years until he died in 1884, Father Doe was one of the pillars of the town. In 1880, he was elected to the legislature and in 1881, he was chosen Speaker of the House. He was president of the Idaho Springs bank and owned two houses, one for revenue. The large bargeboard trimmed frame house in which they lived was the scene of many a social function written up in the Clear Creek *Miner*. But after 1880, Father Doe refused to support Harvey or pay his debts.

Harvey and I moved to Denver where he ineffectively looked for work. I sold the last of my furniture and clothes to keep us alive. After we were divorced, he drifted off. Evan Morgan said he saw him in Gunnison in 1881 and at the time of Father Doe's death, he was in Antonito, Colorado, with Flora, one of his sisters. After the estate was settled, Mrs. Doe moved back to Oshkosh and Harvey went with her. There, and in Milwaukee, he lived out his life, running a cigar store and acting as a hotel detective, and fulfilling the epithet used about him at the Shoo-Fly, "Mama's Boy."

I could not forget nor forgive the painful, galling humiliation of having to have our baby alone in a mining camp. Save for Jake Sandelowsky I had been without friends, without money, and was disgraced, since my husband's absence was talked about everywhere. Harvey's failure to attend to these primary needs for his own wife and child I could not forgive—my heart was emptied of his image for years.

"I think maybe you're right," I told Jake before the second break with

Harvey. "I've been here in Central City for over two years, and very unhappy ones. I think a change would do me good."

Jake sent me over to Leadville on a visit to see what it was like in December, 1879. At the time, although he had moved to Leadville already, he was back in Blackhawk to talk business with Sam Pelton. I traveled by the Colorado Central narrow gauge from Blackhawk to the Forks and then up to Georgetown. From there I went by stagecoach, over lofty Argentine Pass, through Ten Mile Canyon and into the "Cloud City." The stage coach ride was fifty-six miles and the fare, ten dollars. In Leadville I stayed at the then fashionable Clarendon Hotel, built by W. H. Bush, formerly manager of the Teller House in Central City. It was on Harrison Avenue, right next door to the newly opened Tabor Opera House.

Everyone was talking about Tabor and his gifts to Leadville when they weren't exclaiming about the silver discoveries on Fryer and Breece Hills. The air was full of the wildest conversation and buzzing excitement everywhere you turned, and the camp itself made Central look like a one-horse town.

"Oh, I'm sure something marvelous will happen to me here!" I exclaimed as I surveyed busy Harrison Avenue down its four-block length to the juncture with Chestnut Street.

Concord stages, belated because of the recent heavy snows, were rolling into camp hauled by six-horse teams. Huge freight vans, lumbering prairie schooners and all sorts of buggies and wheeled vehicles were toiling up and down the street, separated from the boardwalk by parallel mounds of snow piled in the gutter three and four feet deep. Everywhere was noisy activity, even lot jumping and cabin-jumping, since the population that year had grown from 1,200 to 16,000!

The boardwalks on each side of the street were filled with a seething mass of humanity that had sprung from every quarter of the globe and from every walk of life. Stalwart teamsters jostled bankers from Chicago. Heavy-booted grimy miners, fresh from underground workings, shared a walk with debonair salesmen from Boston. The gambler and bunco-steerer strolled arm in arm with their freshest victim picked up in a hotel lobby.

I had bought "The Tourist Guide to Colorado and Leadville," written by Cass Carpenter in May of that year. The pamphlet said that at the time of writing Leadville had "19 hotels, 41 lodging houses, 82 drinking saloons, 38 restaurants, 13 wholesale liquor houses . . . 10 lumber yards, 7 smelting and reduction works, 2 sampling works for testing ores, 12 blacksmith shops, 6 livery stables, 6 jewelry stores, 3 undertakers and 21 gambling houses where all sorts of games are played as openly as the Sunday School sermon is conducted."

As I now regarded the town, this description seemed to me to be already outdated and the camp to be three times as built up as the guide said.

H. A. W. Tabor, who had been elected Leadville's first mayor and first postmaster, had also organized its first bank. The building stood at the corner of Harrison Avenue and Chestnut, a two-story structure with the design of a huge silver dollar in the gable. The First National Bank, the Merchants and Mechanics Bank and the Carbonate National had also been built. Tabor had already erected a building to house the Tabor Hose Co. (for which he had given the hose carriage) and the equipment of the Tabor Light Cavalry, which he had also organized. Two newspaper offices were already built and a third was preparing to start publishing in January.

"What do you think of our camp?" a stranger said to me somewhat later, accosting me in the lobby of the Clarendon.

I no longer resented the efforts of men to pick me up. Two years in Colorado mining camps had taught me some of the carefree friendliness of the atmosphere. I knew now it wasn't considered an insult.

"Oh, it's wonderful!" I answered, "and has such a beautiful setting."

"Yes, those are marvelous peaks over there, Massive and Elbert—it's a stunning country. I've never seen anything like Colorado. I'm from the South. The man I bunked with was from Missouri. He was scared of the wildness and casual shootings we have around here—so he took one look at that sign over there and beat it home to Missouri to raise some."

I peered across the street. A feed and supply store had a high false front on which was painted in big letters, HAY $40 A TON.

The idea tickled me and I laughed out loud. As I laughed, a great weight fell from my shoulders. It seemed as if it had been a long time since I had really laughed, almost as if my gayety had been boxed in by the ugly gulches of Blackhawk and crushed in the cramped space of Central. But here the whole atmosphere was wide and different!

The man sat down in a rocking chair beside me in the lobby and was soon entertaining me with the many colorful stories of the camp, of the wild nights where everyone whooped it up till dawn, in the saloons, in the variety theatres, in the gambling houses, in the dance halls, in the bagnios and in the streets, milling from door to door.

He also told me of the unusual characters of the town, all the way from the popular Tabor who was Leadville's leading citizen down to "the waffle woman" who could be seen any night regularly at twelve o'clock going from saloon to saloon and from dance house to gambling and other dens selling hot waffles. He had stopped her once and spoken to her. She had replied in a cultured voice:

"My best trade is between two and three in the morning after the theatres are out. It is not pleasant being out so late among so rough a class as is found on the streets after midnight and about the saloons. I have led a pleasanter life. Should I tell you who I am and what I have been, you would not believe me . . ."

His tales fascinated me. But his stories of Tabor and Augusta, Tabor's severe New England wife with whom he was not getting along, interested me more than any others. Tabor, he said, could be seen almost any evening he was in camp in the lobby or across the street in the Board of Trade which was the gambling house and saloon that got most of the after-theatre trade from the Tabor Opera House, opened a month before in November. Tabor was a splendid poker player and was fond of gambling of all sorts. Since he had made so much money in the last two years, he had started playing roulette for enormous stakes.

"Every night?" I asked. "What does Mrs. Tabor do?"

"Don't know—she's down in Denver. But he's gone pretty wild lately. She

33

don't like it and I guess nags him terrible. So he just stays out of her way. He likes his liquor and women, too, and naturally that don't set so good with her. Wouldn't with any wife. But he spends a lot of time on the move nowadays."

"What's he doing in Denver?"

"Oh, he and his right hand man, Bill Bush, are making real estate investments mostly. He's building the Tabor block at 16th and Larimer Streets—costing two hundred thousand dollars—of stone quarried in Ohio. Expects it to be finished in March. And he bought the Henry P. Brown house on Broadway last winter for a residence. Paid $40,000 for it."

"He must be a very great man."

"Some says he is and some says he isn't. I've played poker with him a time or two and he's right smart at that game. But some of the folks around here say he's too fond of show and throwin' his money around. I reckon the Republican politicians trimmed him a heap of money a year ago before they gave him the lieutenant governorship!"

"My, I would love to meet him," I remarked, thinking that never had a description of any man so captured my imagination. "How old is he?"

"Must be right close to fifty. He was one of the early prospectors out here—came in an ox-wagon across the plains in '59. Mrs. Tabor was the first woman in the Jackson Diggings. That's where Idaho Springs is now. He had a claim jumped at Payne's Bar and never done anything about it. An awful easy-going sort of fellow."

Our conversation ran along like this for some time and was continued again in the afternoon. That evening my new friend suggested he take me next door to the Opera House where Jack Langrishe's stock company, brought from New York a month ago, was playing "Two Orphans." He seemed such a pleasant companion and so well-informed on this particular camp and mining in general that I accepted his suggestion with alacrity.

"Thank you very much. I should be delighted and won't you let me introduce myself? I'm Mrs. Doe."

"Not the famous beauty of Central! Most of us miners have already heard about you."

He then introduced himself. But since he is still alive I won't give him away after all these years. We always remained good friends, although on a rather formal basis and never called each other by our first names. In the course of the evening, I asked his opinion about the quartz lodes of Nevadaville, still having in mind that something could be done with Harvey's mine.

"Most of my Colorado mining's been done down in La Plata and San Juan counties. I wouldn't be much help. But my advice to you is to hang on to it and maybe work it on shares with some man in the spring when the snow breaks."

"A new vista for me!" was my reaction. I had always thought of myself as a married woman but now I began to think in terms of a career—I didn't know what. Jake Sands (as he now called himself in order to shorten his name) wanted me to go into business with him when he opened his new clothing store. But in this glamorous, adventurous world it seemed as if that would be too tame a life for a girl whose exotic name had already spread from one mining camp to another.

(I don't mind saying that I was flattered at my new friend's having heard of me—and I am sure that if I hadn't already fallen in love with Leadville, this tribute alone would have persuaded me to change camps.)

When I returned to Central, my mind was made up. I had gone away with a bruised soul, confused and hurt and undecided. My church did not sanction divorce and it was a dreadful wrench to face what such a step would mean.

But the romance of Colorado mining had caught me forever in its mesh— I would never be happy again away from these mountains and away from the gay, tantalizing feeling that tomorrow anything might happen. And did!

Jake Sands was very pleased to see me returning in such good spirits. He helped me from the train at Blackhawk, a smile in the corners of his dark, handsome eyes.

"You look your bright self again. What have you decided—are you going to follow me and desert the Little Kingdom of Gilpin?"

"I think I am, Jake. But wait until I see what mail I have from home and what about Harvey. Then we'll decide."

Christmas letters and gifts had come from all my family, a lovely handsome mohair jacket from Mama, but no word from Harvey in Denver. During the holiday season, I wanted to feel charitable and kind so I put off making any plans. Jake and I celebrated together with his friends at the Shoo-Fly and we had enough jollity and parties to forget my unpleasant domestic situation. I knew that Jake's interest in me was more than just sympathy but he did not broach any word or demand any favors. He was consideration, itself.

When the New Year had passed, I went to Idaho Springs to see the elder Does. Then I went to Denver to find Harvey and tell him I wanted a divorce. He was drinking and we quarrelled again. In response to my request, he said he thought in some ways our marriage had been a mistake. Perhaps if his mother and I hadn't had such religious and other differences, we might have worked it out together. But as it was, couldn't we try again? And he would make me a gift of our Troy Lode mine in which I still believed. Shortly after, he gave me the deed on the back of which he had written in a firm, legible hand:

"I, W. H. Doe, Jr., give up all my rights and title to my claims in the above said property to my wife, Mrs. W. H. Doe, formerly Lizzie B. McCourt of Oshkosh, Wis.

(Signed) W. H. Doe, Jr.
Jan. 29, 1880."

I still wanted a divorce in my heart and, during the winter, inquired about the possibilities of getting one in Arapahoe County. My intention was to sue on the grounds of non-support. But Harvey kept nagging me and, on the night of March 2, wanted to make up. By then, I was so exasperated with his shilly-shallying and so impatient to be free so I could go to Leadville, that I said every cruel thing I could think of. We had a frightful quarrel and he shouted that to spite me, this time he really was going to a sporting house.

"You wouldn't dare!" I snorted. "You aren't that much of a man."

35

He turned on his heel and rushed out of our tiny rooms. I hurried on to the street after him and, at the same time as following Harvey, looked for a policeman. As luck would have it, I found one, Edward Newman, just around the corner. We saw Harvey go into Lizzie Preston's at 1943 Market and we followed him in. There, we got the evidence that I needed for a quick divorce. The decree was granted March 19 and I was ready for a fresh start.

Meanwhile, Jake had been living in Leadville. The night before his going, he had said to me:

"Baby, I have not been without ulterior motive these past months in trying to get you to move on. I hope you will come to Leadville and our friendship can go on the same as ever. That's the place for a girl like you! We might even think of marriage."

I was not in love with Jake, nor did I think I ever should be. But he had been the grandest friend a girl could hope for. I pressed his hand and said with an affectionate smile:

"Perhaps. We'll see."

By the time I reached Leadville, Jake was well established in his clothing business at 312 Harrison Avenue, which was the left-hand front store in the Tabor Opera House. They called this store Sands, Pelton & Co. Jake arranged for me to stay at a boarding house while he lived at 303 Harrison Avenue across the street from his business.

But I suppose once a gambler, always a gambler. Jake never indulged in excessive gambling but the spirit of it was in his blood. He loved to spend an evening, after a hard day's work in the store, satisfying this taste. Instead of the lone Shoo-Fly, there were plenty of places he could go—by now—between forty and sixty alight every night, if you counted the side houses as well as the licensed places.

Pap Wyman's was the most notorious. It stood at State and Harrison. I had been told that every man in camp went there to see the sights, if not to enter into all the activities which under one roof combined liquor-selling, gambling, dancing and woman's oldest profession. The girls wore short skirts with bare arms and shoulders and besides being eager to dance, would encourage men to join them in the "green rooms," a custom taken over from the variety theatres. These were small wine rooms where for every bottle of champagne that a man ordered, the girl's card was punched for a dollar commission.

Frequently, late at night or early in the morning, a "madam" and her retinue of girls from one of the "parlor" houses would swoop into Wyman's to join in the festivities. The dance hall girls were said to envy these "ladies" very much. Their expensive dresses and opulent jewelry, especially as displayed on the madam who was usually a jolly coarse peroxide blonde of forty or fifty, were far beyond their attainments. To be truthful, these sporting women were the aristocracy of the camp since nice married women whose husbands had not found bonanzas, spent the day in backbreaking work at washtubs or over hot stoves and were too tired in the evening to do anything but sleep.

One night Jake had gone over to Wyman's to gamble and I was left to entertain myself. Feeling hungry toward the middle of the evening and being fond of oysters, I crossed Harrison Avenue to the old Saddle Rock Cafe which stood a block down from the Clarendon hotel and Tabor Opera house. When I entered and was shown to a table, the place was rather quiet.

"Intermission yet at the Opera House?" the waiter asked.

"Oh, I don't know," I replied. "I'm not attending tonight. I've already seen this bill . . . 'The Marble Heart'."

"Guess not," he said. "We always get a lively bunch in here then."

I was well aware of this fact. It was one of the reasons I had come. The motley cosmopolitan and rough-neck crowds of Leadville had never ceased to delight me. I could sit for hours in a hotel lobby or a restaurant and ask for no further entertainment than to watch the people.

Just as I finished ordering, the cafe started to fill up and coming in the entrance, I recognized Mr. Tabor with his theatre manager, Bill Bush.

The Silver King!

His tall back had been pointed out to me on the street and in the Clarendon hotel lobby by Jake but I had never before seen him face to face. Both men glanced directly at me where I sat alone at my table, and I saw Mr. Tabor turn toward Mr. Bush to say something. My heart skipped a beat and my oyster fork trembled in my hand.

"The great man of Colorado is talking about me!" ran the thought, vaulting and jubilant, through my mind.

Bush and Tabor were winding up a number of their Leadville affairs, I knew from the papers, because they had leased the Windsor Hotel on Larimer Street in Denver and were planning on opening it as soon as they had completed furnishing the building, probably in June. Tabor's Leadville paper, *The Herald*, kept the camp well informed of their doings and as I was always an avid reader of every item that bore the Tabor name, I felt almost as if I already knew him.

He was over six feet tall with large regular features and a drooping moustache. Dark in coloring, at this time his hair had begun to recede a bit on his forehead and was turning grey at the temples. Always very well and conspicuously dressed, his personality seemed to fill any room he stepped into. His generosity and hospitality immediately attracted a crowd about him and he would start buying drinks and cracking jokes with everyone.

"That's the kind of man I could love," I thought to myself as I bent over my oysters. "A man who loves life and lives to the full!"

At that moment, the waiter tapped me on the shoulder and handed me a note. Scrawled on the back of a theatre program in a refined hand ran the message:

"Won't you join us at our table?
William H. Bush."

The blood rushed into my face and I felt hot and cold. Mr. Bush had been proprietor of the Teller House until a little over a year ago and I had met him with Father Doe when he had taken Harvey and me there for meals. Mr. Bush probably knew my whole humiliating story . . .

Glancing up, my eyes met Mr. Tabor's piercing dark ones across the intervening tables and I knew in an instant that I was falling in love. Love at first sight. Love that was to last fifty-five years without a single unfaithful thought. Almost in a trance, I gathered up my braided gabardine coat and carriage boots to move over to their table.

"Governor Tabor, meet Mrs. Doe who's come from Central to live in Leadville."

I put my hand in Mr. Tabor's large one and it seemed to me as if I never wanted to withdraw it. What was he thinking at that moment, I wondered? Was he feeling the electric magnetism in the touch of my hand as I was in his? Or was I just another one of the women that Augusta Tabor would carp about?

"Sit down, Mrs. Doe, and order anything you want on the menu. No point in going back to the show when we can sit here and entertain as pretty a young woman as you, is there Bill? Here's a little lady we'll have to get to know."

Chapter Three

Leadville, the Saddle Rock Cafe, and the gay, boisterous mining and promoting crowd about me all swam dizzily away from my consciousness as I dropped down in a chair between the great silver king, Horace Tabor, and his manager, Bill Bush. I was in love! That was all I knew.

I was in love with a married man. I, a divorced woman, whose future with Jake was merely a nebulous suggestion. Yet here I was, beside the man I had dreamed of for so long—

"Surely, Bill, we should have champagne on this auspicious occasion?" Mr. Tabor went on.

The evening passed in one of those heavenly hazes in which afterward you want to remember every word, every glance, every happening, yet nothing remains but a roseate glow. We stayed there at the table, laughing and talking and drinking. Mostly we gossiped about people in Central City that Mr. Tabor and I knew of in common—Judge Belford, George Randolph and so on—or else about the operating conditions at the various mines there that I had heard talked about.

But there was one person whose name I never spoke—Jacob Sands. I wondered how much Bill Bush knew—or what he thought he knew. But nothing of this was hinted by either of us.

When the performance across Harrison Avenue at the Tabor Opera House was finished, Bill Bush excused himself, saying:

"I have some accounts to go over before I turn in — see you in the morning, Governor."

Then the greatest man in Colorado leaned toward me and said:

"Now tell me about yourself."

I gasped and began in little gurgles, but it was very easy talking to him.

Little by little, I told him the whole story of my life as I have recounted it here—the high hopes of my marriage, my great reverence and love of the Colorado mountains, my excitement over the mining world, and finally, since his piercing eyes were not piercing when they looked at me, but soft and mellow and understanding, I told him, rather tearfully about Harvey and Jake, and why I was in Leadville.

"So you don't want to marry Jake Sands—but think you ought to because of the money he's spent helping you out?"

"Yes."

"Well, I tell you what. I've got plenty of money, more'n I know what to do with. Let me give you enough to pay this fellow back and carry you along for a while, Something's bound to turn up."

This dazzling offer resounded in my ears like the explosion of dynamite.

"Why, Governor Tabor, I couldn't let you do that!"

"Why not? Look on it as a grubstake. I've grubstaked hundreds of people in my day. Most of 'em came to nothing but some of 'em turned out lucky. I'm a great believer in the Tabor Luck—and this just might be another lucky grubstake for me. No telling."

"But I never met you before this evening!"

"What's that got to do with it? I never saw Hook or Rische before one morning they walked in the old Tabor store and asked me for a grubstake. And then they found the Little Pittsburgh. Meant millions for me!"

"But this grubstake can't mean millions—I'll never be able to repay it to you—"

"Not in money, perhaps. But I'm not looking for money anymore. I want other things out of life, too. You take this grubstake and forget it."

He took a pencil from his pocket and wrote out a draft for five thousand dollars.

"You give this to Bill Bush in the morning and he'll see that you're all fixed up."

As I stared at the sum on the slip of paper, I couldn't believe my eyes. I gulped and glanced up, awe-struck.

"You'll need some clothes and things, too," he explained in a sort of an aside, and then turning to the waiter, called out "Another bottle of champagne, here!"

The merriest night of my life was on. Nobody in Leadville in those days went to bed until nearly dawn. I had been supposed to meet Jake at midnight in the lobby of the Clarendon for a late supper, but in the giddy exhilaration of the evening, I had forgotten all about it. It was way past midnight, now. There was nothing to do—Jake had been a marvelous friend, so marvelous that I never could think of him again without a little twinge of conscience—but I was in love! You can't explain it—yet if you are in love, nothing else seems important. Everything else but your state of heart is out of focus. I would never have met Horace Tabor if it hadn't been for Jake. Yet at that moment, I never wanted to see Jake Sands again.

And I seldom did. Although we often crossed on the streets of Leadville briefly, until he moved to Aspen in 1888, we were only casual friends. In Aspen,

I was later told, he opened another store, married, and bought a house that still stands.

The next morning, after a conference with Bill Bush and Horace Tabor, they decided the best thing to do was to write him an explanatory letter.

"But, Governor Tabor," I said, "Don't you think I ought to see him? He's been such a good friend—I think I ought to talk to him. It would be kinder."

"No, I don't think so. His feelings are bound to be hurt in any case. The quicker, the easier for him in the long run—you can tell him that in your letter. He's a tenant of mine and a nice fellow. Later on, after you've written the letter, we will ask him to dinner some night."

I pondered a long time over the writing of it, and stressed how deeply appreciative I was. I said I had decided not to marry him and I enclosed a thousand dollars which was more than enough to pay off my indebtedness. Even the enclosure of the money I tried to make especially kind.

"Now, Bill, you take this around personally and square Mrs. Doe off right with him," Horace Tabor said. "We don't want to have any hurt feelings around that last. We all want to be friends."

He leaned over and patted my hand in reassurance of my act. But I needed no reassurance once the act was accomplished. My heart was dancing wildly!

History books will tell you the story of my love affair after that. Jake refused the money but did accept the gift of a diamond ring. Tabor moved me from the small room that I had into a suite at the Clarendon, and we became sweethearts.

For me, it was like suddenly walking into the door of heaven. This great man was the idol of whom I had dreamed and whom I had hoped Harvey Doe might copy. In those bleak months in Central City, I had avidly searched out reports of his accomplishments in the newspapers and memorized every word.

After the bonanza strike in the Little Pittsburgh, everything Tabor touched had turned to sparkling silver and untold riches. By the end of 1879, the total yield from the consolidated company was four million dollars and Tabor had sold his interest in this group of mines for a million dollars.

Late in the year before, in partnership with Marshall Field of Chicago, he bought the Chrysolite along with some auxiliary claims. Not long after, these mines had yielded three million dollars and Tabor eventually sold out his share for a million and a half. At the time, they told a story around Leadville about the Chrysolite that was written up in verse and printed on a broadside. They said that "Chicken Bill" Lovell, a clever swindler, had "high-graded" some ore from the Pittsburgh and "salted' the Chrysolite, then a barren hole, owned by Lovell. When Lovell showed his spurious mine to Tabor, the new silver king bought the holding for nine hundred dollars and shortly after put a crew to work. The miners discovered the deception and asked Tabor what to do.

"Keep on sinking," was his command.

Ten feet more and they broke into a three million treasure chest of carbonate ore!

It was also in 1879 that he had bought the Matchless for over a hundred and seventeen thousand dollars and had purchased a half interest in the First National Bank in Denver During the last year, he started expanding his invest-

LIZZIE M'COURT'S GIRLHOOD HOME IN OSHKOSH

Baby Doe was a fat adolescent of sixteen years when this photo was taken in Oshkosh in 1871. She is standing on the verandah, first figure on the left, surrounded by all the members of her family except Mark who was not born until the next year. Her mother and father are standing beside Willard, held on the rocking horse. Her favorite little sister, Claudia, is seated on the steps, and Philip and Peter are standing at the right. Mr. George Cameron, her father's partner, is posed in the buggy. This fine house, 20 Division Street, burned in 1874.

MRS. HARVEY DOE

The Oshkosh Times reported that the wedding of Lizzie McCourt and Harvey Doe at St. Peter's was so crowded that people were standing outside. This photo was taken by A. E. Rinehart in Denver in 1880 at 1637 Larimer Street after their marriage had failed and Baby Doe wanted a divorce.

CLEAN-UP AFTER A FLASH FLOOD IN BLACKHAWK

After Harvey Doe messed up the management of his father's Fourth of July mine at Central City, the young couple took rooms in the brick building above the white circled windows. The trains to Central City chugged over the trestle almost at their bedside. The building, unused, still stands; also Jacob Sands' store, which is just off the photo to the left.

HARVEY DOE

Taken in the late 1890s, this photo came from his step-son, Sam Kingsley of San Diego. Harvey married a widow with three children in 1893. At the time he was a cigar maker in Oshkosh. Later he became a hotel detective in Milwaukee. He died in 1921 and lies there with Ida Doe.

LIZZIE MOVED TO LEADVILLE'S CLARENDON HOTEL

The Clarendon was built on Harrison Avenue in 1879 by William Bush. Soon after, Tabor built the opera house to the left and the two were connected by a catwalk from the top floor. Tabor had rooms and offices upstairs in the opera house and could pass quickly and privately across to Baby Doe's suite. Jacob Sands' store was the one with white awnings downstairs in Tabor's building. Could the caped figure be Lizzie?

NEW SWEETHEART

This photo was taken in Leadville in 1880 and was Tabor's favorite. He had a frame made for it of the finest minted silver from the Matchless mine and kept the photo on his dressing table. In the '90s, he borrowed money on his treasure to buy groceries, but died before it was redeemed.

AUGUSTA

BABY DOE

HORACE

THE TABOR TRIANGLE

When Tabor was forty-seven years old, he struck it rich. He wanted to have a good time, give parties, gain public office, and live in the grand manner. Augusta, his austere New England wife, disapproved; but when gay, smiling Baby Doe applauded a triangle was expertly drawn.

THE WINDSOR HOTEL IN DENVER

The most elegant hostelry of the Rocky Mountain region opened its doors in June, 1880, furnished and run by Tabor and Bush. Very soon its red plush lobby was the gathering place of all the elite and it was not long afterward that Tabor decided to install Baby Doe in one of its suites. She moved from Leadville and took up life close to her lover. Except for the porte-cocheres, the Windsor looked the same until 1958.

GOLD CHAIRS

Central City's Teller House is now the proud owner of these chairs and jewel box that once belonged in Baby Doe's suite at the Windsor. Her diamond necklace contained stones that were said to be Isabella's and was imported from Spain, costing $75,000.

THE TABOR GRAND THEATRE ON OPENING DAY

In September, 1881, Denver had grown to a city of over thirty-five thousand population and it welcomed this handsome and lavish addition to its business buildings with a deep gratitude and much publicity.

DENVER'S GIFT TO TABOR

A ceremony took place the opening night, presenting this watch-fob to Tabor. It represents an ore bucket of nuggets, leading by gold ladders up to the Tabor Store at Oro, the Tabor Block, and last to the Tabor Grand Theatre; the whole depicting the recipient's climb to fame and fortune. On the reverse side, were the date, monograms in enamel and legends, "Presented by the citizens of Denver to H. A. W. Tabor" and "Labor Omnia Vincet." After Baby Doe was found dead, this gold ornament appeared among her things, rolled up in rags. Although she had sold most of her jewels to fulfill Tabor's wish that she hang on to the Matchless, she saved the talisman.

GRANDEUR

Cherry wood from Japan and mahogany from Honduras made the interior of the Tabor subject matter for copious columns of newsprint. The shimmering, expensive crystal chandelier has not yet been hung in this photo; nor the chairs yet placed in the ornate boxes. On opening night they were filled with the cream of Denver society, and reporters' pencils were busy recording the bustles and bangles that made each gown chic or very distinctive.

SCANDAL

Box A was empty on the opening night because Augusta was not invited by her husband. Tongues wagged freely about a Dresden figure, heavily veiled, at the rear. After Baby Doe married Tabor, the box was always decorated with white lilies when she was to be present. The box also bore a large silver plaque, inscribed with the name TABOR.

GLAMOROUS WEDD

When Baby Doe married T
1883, no expense was spared
occasion memorable. A room of
Hotel in Washington, D. C., u
for supper. The centerpiece
high—a wedding bell of whit
mounted by a heart of red roses
by an arrow of violets, shot fro
bow of heliotrope. Other elab
tions garlanded the rest of the
bride wore a $7,000 outfit
lingerie, and a brocaded satin go
in marabou. President Arthur,
congressmen attended the cerem
wives did not, refusing to forg
affair and banning the Tabors
The gown is now in the St

THE BRIDE'S BEAUTY WAS CELEBRATED AFAR

Her reddish gold hair, of which she had masses, was worn in a large
chignon at the nape of her neck until about a year before she married
Tabor. She frizzed the front hair for a fluffy effect; but later she wore the

March,
ke the
Willard
corated
ix feet
es, sur-
pierced
Cupid's
decora-
n. The
al lace
rimmed
ors and
ut their
e illicit
society.
useum.

back hair high and had the whole elaborately curled. Many men succumbed to her charm and looks; among them, Carl Nollenberger, popular Leadville saloon keeper, who had a beer tray made, portraying her dainty profile. Her earlier photos have naturally arching eyebrows; but later she pencilled these blacker and straighter. She preferred color; the black is mourning for her father who died May, 1883. By then, she had also had her ears pierced.

BABY DOE TABOR'S DREAM HOUSES

The second house that Tabor bought was on the south side of 13th and ran from Grant to Sherman. Shown are Tabor with his favorite horse and Baby Doe beside a disputed statue. Three of the scandalous nude figures can be seen, too, at the left by the spruce tree and in the center of the pool. The interior shows a playing fountain, crystal chandelier, heavy walnut furniture, oriental rugs and hangings, oil paintings, mirrors, a loaded buffet, silver pitcher and every sort of bric-a-brac, dear to those of the Victorian era.

THE FIRST BORN

No baby had such lavish belongings and such wide attention as Lillie Tabor, who was born in July, 1884. Her christening outfit cost $15,000. Her mother, who was fond of keeping scrapbooks, entered many clippings about her beautiful baby. The right-hand page contains three clippings from January, 1887, describing the visit of the artist, Thomas Nast, to Denver and his sketching the baby for Harper's Bazaar. When Lillie was eighteen, she ran away to McCourt relatives in Chicago. Later she married her cousin, John Last, and settled in Milwaukee. Her daughters, Caroline and Jane, resided there for some years after Lillie's death in 1946, concealing their Tabor descent.

SILVER DOLLAR

Baby Doe lost her second baby, a boy; and her third child, born in 1889, was another little girl. She only enjoyed four years of the rich, petted life that her sister had had. Christened a long string of names, she used Silver and Silver Dollar the most. Although Lillie resembled Baby Doe in looks, Silver, who had the nickname of "Honeymaid," was closer to her mother. Silver spent most of her adolescence and young womanhood in Leadville, living with her mother at assorted cheap locations. She was fond of horses, gay parties, dancing and excitement.

* * *

Baby Doe's favorite daughter tried to be a newspaper woman, a movie actress, and a novelist with one printed book, "Star of Blood." But she failed in all her ventures. Silver Dollar's end was tragic and sordid in the extreme. She was scalded to death under very suspicious circumstances in a rooming house in Chicago's cheapest district. Not yet thirty-six years old, she was a perpetual drunk, was addicted to dope and had lived with many men under several aliases. Her funeral expenses were paid by Peter McCourt.

* * *

MEETING "T. R."

Baby Doe's happiest moment about Silver was this one, recorded on August 29, 1910, when the ex-president Roosevelt was visiting in Denver and received a song about his former visit with lyrics signed by Silver Echo Tabor, age 20, a pretty brunette.

So fleet the works of men, back to the earth again,
Ancient and holy things fade like a dream.
— Kingsley

THE PROPHETIC CURTAIN AND ITS FATAL WORDS

The Tabors lived opulently and showily right up to the moment of the Silver Panic in 1893 when their fortune came tumbling down. In the same year, 1895, that Augusta died a wealthy woman in California, they were bankrupt. Tabor became a day laborer and Baby Doe did the hardest sort of manual work. Finally Tabor was appointed postmaster of Denver. The Tabors and their two little girls moved into two rooms at the Windsor and here they lived until Tabor's death in 1899. His dying words to Baby Doe were, "Hang on to the Matchless. It will make millions again." But the people of Denver, attending performances in the Tabor Theatre, looked at the curtain and quoted Kingsley's sad couplet:

"So fleet the works of men, back to the earth again,
"Ancient and holy things fade like a dream."

THE MATCHLESS MINE BECAME BABY DOE'S HOME

For nearly thirty-six years after Tabor's death, Baby Doe followed her husband's injunction. Between leases, and sometimes during leases, she lived in a small tool cabin beside the shaft and the hoist house. At the time of the author's visit, in 1927, the mine looked as above. This shot is taken looking west, in the direction of Leadville, and a spur of Fryer Hill is blocking a view of the continental divide. Baby Doe furnished the cabin (at the left) with plain furniture and subsisted on cheap edibles. But the cabin was always extremely neat and her coal and wood in tidy piles. Below is one of the last pictures taken of her, October 6, 1933, and shows her characteristic clothing. In winter, she wrapped her feet in burlap.

FORTUNE HUNTERS

After Baby Doe's body was found frozen, March 7, 1935, vandals entered her cabin, ransacked her belongings, ripping up the mattress and overturning everything, while they tried to find a fortune they imagined she had hidden. But all the effects, that had been preserved from her glorious days, were with the nuns or in Denver warehouses. Baby Doe, herself, was neat and tidy.

JACOB SANDS' HOUSE IN ASPEN

Baby Doe's friend bought a cottage at Hunter and Hopkins in 1889 and later he rented this house on Main Street. Both his residences still stand and are the delight of the tourists. In 1898, he and his wife and their children moved to Leadville, then Arizona, and are now lost to history.

THE ETERNAL SNOWS VIEWED FROM FRYER HILL

When Baby Doe walked to town by the road that led into Leadville's Eighth Street, this was the view that faced her across the Arkansas Valley. The mountains are miles away but seem close in the rarified atmosphere. They are Elbert (Colorado's highest) to the left and Massive to the right. Below is the Matchless Mine after its partial restoration in 1953.

ments far and wide—towards an iron mine on Breece Hill, gold mines in the San Juans, silver mines in Aspen, placer mines in Park county, smelters, irrigating canals, toll roads, railroads, copper land in Texas, grazing lands in Southern Colorado, a huge land concession in Honduras, and real estate in Leadville, Denver and Chicago.

Now, in the shadow of the Continental Divide, this man, this Croesus, had become my lover. I just knew those gorgeous mountains would answer my prayer that first morning I saw them!

Meanwhile, Mrs. Tabor and Horace were entertaining society in their fine house in Denver and I only saw him on his visits to Leadville. But these visits were frequent, because that was the year of the fires in the Chrysolite mine and the strike that finally turned out all the miners of the district. Leadville was bedlam in June. Knots of men were loitering around everywhere, or preventing other miners from entering town, and the whole temper of the streets very ugly. Strikers and mine-owners both grew increasingly obstinate.

The strikers were most virulently angry against Tabor. Everyone went armed and the tenseness of the situation seemed about to destroy my new-found happiness. The miners said Tabor had been one of them just a short time ago, and it was their vote that had put him in political power. Now he had forgotten.

"Dirty B———, to turn on us," I overheard many of the men in the street muttering.

Something had to be done. Tabor was one of the property owners to organize a Committee of Safety. They met with dramatic secrecy in Tabor's private rooms in the Opera House, and after drawing up an agreement similar to that of the Vigilance Committee of early San Francisco, elected C. C. Davis, the editor of the Chronicle, their leader. Mr. Davis first sounded out Governor Pitkin on declaring martial law, but he said to call on him only as a last resort.

Feeling climbed to a higher pitch. Seven committees of local militia were organized and tempers were now reaching the boiling point. One day on Harrison Avenue for a distance of eight blocks, eight thousand striking miners menacingly swaggered back and forth and a like number of citizens of opposite sympathies paraded with determination as grim as theirs. The street was jammed. As I looked down, worried and fearful, from the window of my suite, it seemed as if at any moment, a local war would break out and the whole camp be destroyed by flames and bloodshed.

The leading men of the town took this moment to read a proclamation to the miners. Tabor, Davis and a number of others stepped out on the balcony of the Tabor Opera House. I hurried into the street to watch the proceedings, my heart beating wildly with fear. The seething mass of humanity below these men were all armed and they were mostly good shots. Tabor standing up so tall and dark and fierce on the balcony would make an excellent target.

"Oh, dear God," I prayed. "Don't let anything happen!"

I hardly realized I was praying at the time. But Davis demanded menacingly that the strike be called off. He told the miners to return to work, then said that if they would not accede, the citizens would protect the owners.

He said they would bring in other workers to take their jobs. My fear was so great that I could actually hear my lips mumbling incoherent, beseeching words.

A shot rang out!

The sharp noise seemed to rend my heart in two. I hardly dared take my eyes from the balcony to glance around for fear of missing a falling figure among that intrepid group. But Tabor and his friends were straight and unconcerned. Their belief in law and order made them brave. The cut-throat mob must have sensed that. No figure fell from their midst. Whatever the shot was, it had not been fired at them. I sighed with relief.

Colonel Bohn of the Committee of Safety was trying to urge a horse he was mounted on through the mob, and was brandishing a drawn sword to emphasize his right. It was a very foolish thing to do at a time like that.

"Somebody must be trying to shoot the old fool," the teamster next to me in the crowd remarked.

"Maybe a signal for the miners to start firing," the man with him offered as a counter-suggestion.

I was terrified—not for myself—but because of Tabor's exposed position. My hands flew to my throat.

"Oh, don't say that!" I almost screamed.

The teamster turned around and stared at me.

"You're all right—they won't shoot you. It's them damned slave-driving millionaires they're after."

And Tabor was the one they were after most! But nothing happened. A policeman pulled Colonel Bohn off his horse and rushed him to the jail "for disturbing the peace," although it was more likely for safe-keeping. Finally, both sides of the fray began to split up in little groups, then to disperse and go home. The immediate danger was over. But I knew now what it was like to be in love with a prominent man in an important political office. It meant helpless fear of an assassin's bullet. And fear was a new emotion to me—that's where love had brought me. I shuddered and turned inward to the Clarendon.

Martial law was declared some hours later and slowly the miners went back to work, having lost their cause. There was covert grumbling in the saloons and on the streets for some time, but at last, life got back to normal, and the regular hum of the pumps at all the mines around filled the night again.

That July, ex-President Grant came to Leadville for a ten-day visit in and about the mining country. He came as Tabor's guest and Tabor, as lieutenant-governor, headed a committee sent down to meet the general's private car. It was coming on the D.&R.G. tracks from Manitou where the great man and his wife had been taking the waters. The committee accompanied the presidential party into camp over a road lighted the last miles with enormous bonfires. I was very thrilled at the idea of the President actually being in my hotel. After he had toured the mines and smelters and addressed discharged soldiers from the Civil War, a banquet was given him at the Clarendon on the last of his three days in the town proper.

The luxuriousness of the scene was impressive. The *Leadville Chronicle* was printed on white satin to give to the President at the banquet as a souvenir of his visit. The gift made such a tremendous impression on him that when he died, he willed it to the Smithsonian Institution in Washington where it may still be seen.

Tabor, rather bewildered and shame-faced, came to me afterward in our suite and said:

"Darling, I know the President wanted to meet you more than anyone else in Leadville. I saw him look at you several times—you are always the most beautiful woman in any gathering. But you know this mining camp and how it talks. We must be discreet."

"Yes, I understand perfectly,"—and I leaned over and kissed his forehead. He had thrown himself down rather disconsolately in a big overstuffed chair, and now he gathered me into his lap. We were locked in each other's embrace for some minutes. We were happy just to be together.

When our relationship first began, I'm sure I was the most in love. But all through the summer, Tabor had begun to talk to me more and more seriously. Though he talked mostly about mining matters and about his political ambitions, he spoke finally about Augusta and me. It was an enormous experience, touching me to the soul, to watch the unfolding of the love and trust of the man I adored.

At first, I had been hardly more than a pretty toy of which he was very fond. He would lavish all sorts of costly presents on me—jewelry, clothes, and that rarest and most extravagant tribute in a mining camp at 10,000 feet altitude, flowers.

I remember one day he sent up a woman who used to peddle hand-made underwear across the mountains from camp to camp. She carried her samples and some of her wares in a large bag she packed on her back. Tabor sent her up to my suite one day. Then when she had everything in the way of exquisite lace and embroidered chemises laid out over the chairs and bed, he joined us and bought me over $350 worth of her goods!

But now things were different, I didn't hear so many stories about his other women. I could feel his love for me growing with the appreciation he had for my character.

"You're always so gay and laughing, Baby," he would say, "and yet you're so brave. Augusta is a damned brave woman, too, but she's powerful disagreeable about it."

He would sit glum and discouraged for a while, and then add:

"And I can't imagine a woman who doesn't like pretty things! I've tried to buy her all sorts of clothes and jewelry since we've had the money. But she just throws them back in my face and asks me if I've lost my mind."

You can hear it said and you can read it in books that I broke up Governor Tabor's home, and that he broke up mine. But that is far from the truth. Both of our marriages had failed before we ever met.

Augusta Tabor had no capacity for anything but strenuous work and very plain living. When they moved into their palatial new home, she wouldn't live upstairs in the master's bedroom but moved down in the servants' quarters off the kitchen. She said they were plenty good enough for her—and how could she cook all that way away from the stove? She also insisted on keeping a

43

cow tethered on the front lawn and milking it, herself. Tabor was very humiliated by these actions. As lieutenant-governor of the state, he was very anxious to live in a style befitting his station. Also, he hoped to be senator.

But Augusta Tabor laughed at his ideas in a very mean way. Tabor had a really sweet disposition. He would come to me often to tell me of some upsetting incident, with a dreadfully hurt look in his eye. Another trait of Tabor's that irritated Augusta tremendously was his generosity. Anybody could touch Tabor for sizable loans · with no trouble at all. He was delighted to help people less fortunate than he.

He had always been like that, and he was to the day he died. When he was Leadville's first postmaster, he made up out of his own pocket the salaries of some five employees just so that Leadville could have more efficient service. He gave money to every church in Leadville for their building fund regardless of the denomination. He gave money for the Tabor Grand Hotel in Leadville (now the Vendome) in 1884, even after he moved away. He was the same lovable donor when he moved to Denver.

He sold the land at the corner of Sixteenth and Arapahoe Streets to the city of Denver for a postoffice, at a bargain price, and he followed this gesture up with a hundred and one donations to private and public charities.

"Trying to buy your way to popularity," Augusta would sniff disparagingly.

Tabor would wince under her barbs. He gave because he liked people. He was naturally friendly, and the only times he gave money, hoping for some definite return, were in political channels. All his other gifts were spontaneous. But Augusta did not understand this generosity and she didn't like it. And what Augusta did not like, she could make exceedingly clear with her sharp tongue! He never was her husband after July, 1880.

Naturally, in these trying circumstances, Tabor turned more and more to me. Later, that fall, he suggested that he should re-furnish one of the suites at the Windsor and that I should move to Denver to be closer to him. Nothing could have thrilled or delighted me more.

"Oh, darling! I would adore to live at the Windsor," I cried, throwing my arms around him.

The Windsor was the last word in elegance, with a sixty-foot mahogany bar, a ballroom with elaborate crystal chandeliers, and floor of parquetry, and a lobby furnished in thick red carpet and diamond-dust-backed mirrors. It was much more impressive than the old American House, which had thrilled my girlish heart when I had first come to Colorado. Here was my dream slowly unfolding before me, almost exactly as I had first visualized it—to be a queen in the cosmopolitan circles of Denver!

Later we departed for Denver separately. I took the Rio Grande and wore a heavy veil. He took the stagecoach over to South Park and then went on the rival narrow gauge in David Moffat's private car. But our reunion at the Windsor was all the more delightful because of our enforced separation. After Augusta's comments on the Leadville strike, Tabor never spent an evening up on Broadway, but came to me more and more often.

"You're a vulgar boor—I've always known that," she had said, "but at least I thought you had enough sense not to call a common lynching gang a Committee of Safety for Law and Order. And getting mixed up with that silly egotistic rooster, Davis, who used a six-shooter for a gavel! And forcing Governor Pitkin to declare martial law. Mark you my words, you've lost all the political popularity you've been so busy buying by your recent actions."

Tabor was very hurt at this, the more so because there seemed to be an element of truth in her words. The attitude toward him in Leadville had changed and Tabor really loved that mining camp—it was always "home" to him, much more than Denver. And in later years, I felt the same way, although just then I was eager to conquer fresh fields.

"Never mind," I said. "I'm sure she's wrong—and besides what do you care about that ugly old mining camp? You're a big man going to do the biggest things for the nation. And what if Governor Pitkin doesn't like you? Probably next election, you'll be governor, yourself!"

Meanwhile, Tabor busied himself with plans for building another opera house, The Tabor Grand, in Denver. He called in his architects, W. J. Edbrooke and F. P. Burnham (who had designed the Tabor Block) and stuffed their pockets with $1,000 notes.

"Go to Europe and study the theatres of London, Paris, Berlin and Vienna. Pick up any good ideas they've got laying around and improve on them. I want only the best!"

Besides the architects, Tabor sent other agents on various missions. He detailed one man to go to Brussels for carpets, another to France for brocades and tapestries, a third to Japan for the best cherry wood to make the interior woodwork, a fourth to Honduras for mahogany for other trimming. A dozen contracts were drawn up in New York and Chicago for furnishings and fripperies. The building would be the most expensive west of the Mississippi.

About this time, Tabor went back to Leadville on a spree that Bill Bush was careful to tell me about. Bill had begun to feel jealous of my influence with Tabor although we were still outwardly very good friends. He wanted to make me jealous, in turn.

Tabor borrowed Dave Moffat's private car and went to Leadville for a ball that the fast women and sports of the town were giving in the Wigwam. He told me and, undoubtedly, Augusta, that he had to go up to Leadville on some mining business and would probably be gone several days.

The ball turned out to be an orgy. Everyone drank too much and Tabor was supposed to have stumbled about with a girl in a gaudy spangled gown which, a few days before the ball, had been on display in the window of the Daniels, Fisher and Smith Dry Goods Emporium on Harrison Avenue, Leadville, bearing a tag marked $500. Bill Bush tried to insinuate that Tabor had bought it as a gift to another one of his loves.

"And why shouldn't he, Bill?" I asked. "I love the man as he is. You forget I'm not Augusta. If he wants to have a good time among his friends, I think that's fine. He knew all of them a long time before he knew me."

But Bill wouldn't believe I was sincere. He replied:

"Well, you're a good actress!"

Then he added some more juicy details. After the ball, those who could still walk trooped over to the Odeon Variety Theatre where a new show started at 3 a.m. Tabor had sat in a box smoking cigars and drinking champagne. Every time he thought a girl was especially attractive, he would throw a shower of gold and silver coins over her head. At the intermission he had invited the actresses into his box and put his arms about their neat waists.

After the show ended at five o'clock, he went to the Saddle Rock Cafe, our favorite restaurant, for breakfast. Then he went back to the Clarendon, finally, to sleep. He slept all the next day. In the evening he asked three or four successful mining men to accompany him back to Denver in the private car. Having slept all day, he sat up all night as the train climbed over Kenosha Pass, playing poker, using twenty-dollar gold pieces as chips.

"And why shouldn't he? I like a gambling man—someone who isn't afraid to take chances—that was one of the worst faults of Harvey Doe."

Bill Bush shrugged his shoulders. Presently he laughed off the whole conversation with:

"You're a clever girl, Baby—shrewd as they come! But talking about your late and not too much lamented husband, where is he and what's the state of your divorce? The Governor wants me to find out."

"I don't know where Harvey is but my divorce is final—I got it a year ago and I am a completely free agent."

The year was now 1881. All that spring and summer, Tabor and I were immersed in the planning and erection of the great building that was to be a monument to the Tabor name for all time. Tabor had left home unequivocally in January, but as he was on so many frequent trips to New York, Chicago or Leadville, where he stayed was really not noticed until that autumn.

At the festive opening night of the Tabor Grand Opera House, with Emma Abbott singing Lucia, Box A of the six fashion boxes was conspicuously empty. That was the box Tabor had reserved for himself and family. It was wreathed in flowers and a huge pendant of roses hung above it. He was on the stage or in the wings waiting for the ceremony of dedication. Augusta, alone of all elaborately gowned Denver society, did not put in an appearance. I could hear whispers all around.

"Look, Mrs. Tabor isn't here! Probably she's found out about that blonde! Wonder if the little hussy's had the nerve to come. . . ."

I was there, but veiled and sitting in an inconspicuous seat in the parquet. I was right where I could see Tabor's son, Maxcy, in Box H with Luella Babcock of whom his father had told me he was very fond, and the sight made me both happy and worried. I was happy to be there on an occasion so memorable to the great man I loved. But I was worried and unstrung about what would be the outcome of our love.

Augusta did know about me, because Bill Bush had been sent to her to try to negotiate a divorce a short time after Bill had looked up the record of my proceedings. But Augusta was obdurate. She considered divorce a lasting disgrace and stigma. She had refused pointblank. And so without a bid from Tabor that tremendous night of September 5, 1881, she stayed home.

The newspapers of Denver devoted pages to the opening and dedication. Even Eugene Field who ordinarily poked a great deal of unkind fun at Tabor in his capacity as an editor of the *Denver Tribune*, printed a complimentary quatrain:

"The opera house—a union grand
Of capital and labor,
Long will the stately structure stand
A monument to Tabor."

The brick and limestone building, five stories high with a corner tower, was described as modified Egyptian Moresque architecture. It housed stores and offices besides the theatre proper, and all the necessary property and dressing rooms. The auditorium had an immense cut-glass chandelier and a beautiful drop-curtain painted by Robert Hopkin of Detroit. It showed the ruins of an ancient temple with broken pillars around a pool, and bore the following inscription by Charles Kingsley:

"So fleet the works of men, back to the earth again,
Ancient and holy things fade like a dream."

Many writers since that day have pointed out the weird prophecy of Tabor's fortune hidden in those lines. But no one thought anything of the curtain that night except that it was dignified and very decorative. Of course, I had seen the curtain before as I (shrouded in a veil when there were associates or too many workmen about) had spent much time with Tabor going over every detail.

Originally he had planned to have a portrait of Shakespeare hung in the lobby, but I said:

"No. Have your own portrait. *You* are Denver's benefactor."

The next day he had the portrait altered. I also suggested the idea of a large silver plate with gold letters to be hung on Box A. When the jeweler delivered it, the block was two feet long and six inches thick, of solid silver from the Matchless Mine. The name Tabor was in relief letters of solid gold. I thought it was one of the handsomest things I ever saw. But I could spend pages on descriptions of the luxuries and elaborate furnishings of that building—as indeed many writers have already done before me.

But after that night, tongues wagged more venomously. Augusta continued mad and obstinate. It was a very trying situation for Tabor in a political way, as naturally all this defaming talk would have a bad effect on his reputation. Often he would come to me with his troubles. Finally, I suggested:

"Perhaps, If I moved over to the American House and gave you my suite, that would at least stop gossip around the Windsor. Nobody much hangs around the American House, the way they do this lobby."

"Baby, you are wonderful. You are the cleverest little woman in the world! No one knows how much I want to make you my wife. And be able to show you off to the world as the proud man I really am! And not have to hide you behind that hideous veil—but what can I do with Augusta? She won't talk to me and she won't listen to Bill Bush. I haven't given her any money for months now, just to try to force her to listen to reason."

"There must be some way. First, I'll move. You stay here at the Windsor and then we'll see."

"It isn't as if she loved me. She couldn't, and talk to me the way she always has. It's just that she's a dog in the manger—she doesn't want me herself, but, by gad, she'll see to it that you don't get me!"

"Love will find a way," I said encouragingly. My own heart leaped with excitement. Tabor had proposed to me before and told me that he loved me. But I had been afraid to let myself believe entirely in the last complete fulfillment of my dream. I loved the greatest man in Colorado, and he loved me. That was almost enough. Now he wanted me to become his wife! I lifted my mouth to his with new depth and resolution in my soul.

Sometimes when I would be writing home to Mama trying to describe to her all the strange glamour and drama and riches of my new life, I would think of the other side of my existence. That side was not so pretty, for the daughter who had set out as a bride. Harvey Doe was almost as if he'd never been—my whole life was Tabor. Naturally, my letters reflected the truly great love that absorbed me, even if it had to be hidden from the world.

But I knew Mama would understand and love me just the same, and Papa would forgive me when finally Tabor and I were actually married.

Augusta, however, made the first drastic move. She brought suit for a property settlement, and publicly dragged the situation into the limelight. She wanted the courts to compel Tabor to settle $50,000 a year on her and also to give her the home on Broadway as well as some adjoining land.

Her bill of complaint gave a list of his holdings totaling over nine million dollars and said she believed his income to be around $100,000 a year. Meanwhile, she said he had contributed nothing to her support since January, 1881, and she had been compelled to take roomers and boarders into her home to support herself. This was not true. Bill Bush had been told to offer her a very substantial settlement if she would give Tabor a divorce and she already had some money of her own.

"Now I'm mad!" Tabor said to me that night. "Nobody ever called me a stingy man till this minute. And by God, that old termagant will find out I *can* be stingy!"

He had that suit quashed with no difficulty as being without the jurisdiction of the court. But the divorce question was different. The lawyers were deadlocked for months. Augusta wouldn't grant the divorce. In turn, Tabor wouldn't grant her a penny with or without the divorce. I rather encouraged him in this last stand, probably foolishly, but I had seen her hurt him so frequently that when he did turn on her for such an unjust attack, I told him he should fight back. But this battle only delayed my own chance for happiness, and, meanwhile, wasn't doing Tabor's political reputation any good.

"Tabor," I said to him one evening when he came to call at the American House, "I have an idea where we might be a little foxier than Augusta and, if nothing else, frighten her into a different position."

"How's that?" he said glumly—we hardly ever had any fun any more, feeling we had to hide away from people. Besides, most of the time, Tabor was stirred up about Augusta's meanness and obstinacy.

"Well, with all your influence, couldn't you get a divorce in some other county than Arapahoe where you also own property? Maybe it wouldn't be entirely valid. But we could act like it was, and get married. If Augusta knew she was married to a bigamist, maybe she would consider that a worse disgrace than being a divorcee!"

Tabor leaped up out of his chair and charmingly whirled me off my feet and around and around in the room with boyish enthusiasm.

"Baby, I always told you you were wonderful! I know just the place— Durango! I own a mine down there, and the judge is a great friend of mine. I'm sure I can fix it up in no time at all. If we can just keep it secret from everyone but Augusta—and then just flash the decree under her nose— and then our marriage certificate—we'll have her where we want her!"

Meantime, all during the year of 1882, subversive political factions were at work to bring pressure on the legislature of one kind and another. When President Garfield had been shot in July of the year before, Chester Arthur succeeded to his position. President Arthur appointed Senator Henry M. Teller to his cabinet. This left a vacancy in one of Colorado's electoral seats. Governor Pitkin appointed a mediocre politician by the name of George Chilcott to Teller's place only until the legislature should convene.

"Just did that because he wants the office himself and to spite me," Tabor explained.

And I heard this opinion verified frequently by other men. The legislature was not to meet until January of the next year, 1883, when they were to elect two senators, one to fill a six-year term, and the other to the thirty days remaining of Teller's term. Everyone said that Tabor would get the six-year term, even though Governor Pitkin wanted it and had the support of the regular Republican machine. Tabor was so popular.

But Augusta ruined all that. The Durango divorce came through without any hitch in the summer of 1882, and on September 30, Tabor and I met secretly in St. Louis, having gone by different trains. We met in the office of Colonel Dyer, a leading attorney, who summoned John M. Young, a justice of the peace. When we went to the court house to get a license, Tabor took the recorder, C. W. Irwin, aside and fixed it up with him that under no circumstances should our license be included on the list given to the daily press.

"Secretly divorced and secretly remarried," Tabor said that night, elated as a school boy. "That'll be something for Augusta to swallow about the man she thinks she can keep tied down! It's also a good precaution for those scandal mongers at the senate. If they get too nosey, we'll show them we're really married."

I tried to pretend I was as happy as he. But to me, a marriage was only binding when it had been sanctioned by the church and performed by a priest. And I knew Papa would only forgive my transgressions on that basis. I had drifted very far away from much of Father Bonduel's teachings but the kernel still remained. I had offended against many of the Church's mandates and of God's. But I still wanted to be safely back in the fold, living the life of a

49

respectable married woman, devoted to her husband, her children, and her home. With that picture in my mind, I could not join as heartily as I should have wished in the champagne toast Tabor made at a tete-a-tete supper at the old Southern Hotel.

"Here's to our wedding day!" he exclaimed with sincere joviality.

"Yes," I agreed, and added with the fervor of the wish that was gnawing at my heart, "here's to our marriage!"

The New Year of 1883 dawned with both our heads whirling with hopes and fears. Hope ran very high that Tabor would soon be going to Washington for six years and I, with him. Fear besieged us with the thought that Augusta would prevent all this. But two enormous events happened that January.

Augusta sued for divorce and accepted a settlement of their house, the La Veta Place apartment house, and a quarter of a million dollars worth of mining stock, including one half interest in the Tam O'Shanter mine above Aspen. Augusta created a hysterical scene in court, which did Tabor a lot of damage. When the trial was over and she was asked to sign the papers, she turned toward the judge and shrilled in a fearful voice,

"What is my name?"

"Your name is Tabor, ma'am. Keep the name. It is yours by right."

"I will. It is mine till I die. It was good enough 'for me to take. It is good enough for me to keep. Judge, I ought to thank you for what you have done, but I cannot. I am not thankful. But it was the only thing left for me to do. Judge, I wish you would put in the record, 'Not willingly asked for.'"

Augusta rose and began to sniffle in a horrible manner, making a spectacle of herself. Before she reached the door, she broke down in tears and sobbed, "Oh, God, not willingly, not willingly!"

I was not there but many people ran to tell me about it, particularly Bill Bush, who dramatized his sympathy very heavily.

"Well," I said, not feeling in the least sorry for Augusta, "If she really did feel that way, why did she go home to Maine and stay so long that autumn before I met Tabor? That was when she lost him. He had a chance then to find out there were plenty of other women in the world, and what's more important, with better dispositions and nicer looks. Either she should never have left him or else she should have been twice as sweet when she got back."

Reluctantly, Bill agreed with me—he had to admit the truth.

But the newspapers were different. They printed scathing editorials about the whole affair, and intimated that Tabor would be forever damned politically.

They weren't entirely right, but they nearly were. The contest in the legislature was long and bitter. The balloting went on and on and no one could break the deadlock between Pitkin and Tabor. All of a sudden the Pitkin men switched to Bowen, a third candidate, a wealthy mining man from the southern part of the state whom no one had taken seriously up to that time. Out of a clear sky he got the six-year term.

As a sop to Tabor, he was unanimously offered the thirty days remaining of Teller's term. Tabor was always a good sport. He accepted the offer with extraorainary grace under the circumstances, congratulated his rival, and prepared to leave immediately. That was January 27, 1883, and by February 3, he was being sworn in at Washington I have never seen anyone so delighted and happy as Tabor was, leaving Denver. He was fifty-two years old but you would have thought he was twelve and had been given his first pony. I, too, was joyful and expectant.

"And what a wedding we'll have, Baby!" he said in parting. "I'll fix all the details and send for you to be married just before my term is up. If all goes well, you'll have both a priest and a president at your ceremony! A lover couldn't do more.

"But don't tell anyone anything about my plans, or they may go wrong. Get your clothes ready. Write to your family very secretly in Oshkosh to join you in Chicago. I'll have a private car put on there for you just about a week before March 4.

"And you'll be the most beautiful and talked-of bride in the world. Just you wait and see."

Chapter Four

My wedding day! A lavish, historic wedding that was famous around the world and was to be talked of for years to come—that was the marriage I had.

Toward the end of Tabor's thirty-day stay in the senate in Washington, he sent for me. In the meantime, I had left Denver and gone back to Oshkosh to visit my family. Mama was elated with the dazzling good fortune that had befallen me. She wept with excitement and joy; Papa was gradually becoming reconciled to the idea of a second marriage provided the ceremony could be performed by a priest. Tabor wrote he thought he could arrange this.

"I'd certainly like to run smack into Mrs. Doe," Mama sniffed. "Here she thought you weren't good enough for Harvey—and now you're marrying one of the richest men in the United States and may end up living in the White House!"

In some ways, I shared Mama's spitefulness but I was too absorbed in anticipation of my jewelled future to spend much time looking backward. Mama couldn't understand how Tabor and my love for him had completely blotted out everything that had gone before. In fact, I don't think she understood then that I really was in love with Tabor, a man twenty-four years my senior. Later, she learned that I was sincere in this great overwhelming emotion of my life.

Papa and Mama, two of my sisters, two of my brothers and two brothers-in-law arrived at the Willard Hotel the last week in February to be with me. The wedding invitations had quarter-inch silver margins and engraved superscriptions, also in silver. I addressed them in my own handwriting, sending them to President Arthur, Secretary of the Interior and Mrs. Henry M. Teller, Senator and Mrs. Nathaniel P. Hill, Senator-elect Tom Bowen, Judge and Mrs. James Belford (he was Colorado's only congressman at the time), Senator Jerome B. Chaffee and others with Colorado affiliations.

I had them delivered personally by a liveried coachman in the rich victoria which Tabor had engaged for his stay in Washington, and which I, as Miss McCourt, was now using.

"I'm sorry, Miss," the coachman said on his return. "Mrs. Hill said to give you this."

In his hand lay a returned invitation torn vigorously once across.

I blushed but said nothing. In my mind, I resolved that the day would come when Denver society would not be able to insult me like that. After we were married, had traveled in Europe, and were settled in the grand house that Tabor would buy me, they would feel differently. Just let Mrs. Hill who had lived so close to me in Blackhawk wait and see! Maybe her coachman did hire my friend, Link Allebaugh, to drive a wagon filled with her household goods when she moved to Denver and maybe she had seen me with Jake in Sandelowsky-Pelton, but times were different now!

At nine o'clock in the evening of March first, the wedding party assembled in one of the larger of the Willard's parlors. I was gowned in a marabou-trimmed, heavily brocaded white satin dress with real lace lingerie, an outfit that cost $7000. I had hoped to wear Tabor's wedding present to me, a $75,000 diamond necklace which he was having made in New York. It had been sold to him as an authentic part of the jewels Queen Isabella had pawned to outfit Columbus for his voyage to America. My dress was made very decollete so as to show off the necklace to the best advantage, but it was not completed in time, so I omitted jewelry. I wore long white gloves and carried a bouquet of white roses.

My family was in black since they were in mourning because of the recent death of my older brother, James. Mama's and the girls' black silks were relieved, however, by ornaments of diamond and onyx which Tabor had given them. Tabor appeared with Bill Bush and Tom Bowen.

We stood in front of a table richly draped in cardinal-red cloth. It held a candelabra with ten lighted tapers that shed a subdued and religious light over the assemblage. All the men had come, including President Arthur, but none of their wives. I was hurt and disappointed at this turn of events but I didn't let it spoil the sweetness of my smile nor the graciousness of my behavior to any of them.

The ceremony, an abbreviated nuptial mass, was performed by the Reverend P. L. Chapelle of St. Matthew's. When it was over, Tabor kissed me and then President Arthur stepped up to offer his congratulations.

"I have never seen a more beautiful bride," he exclaimed, shaking my hand. "May I not beg a rose from your bouquet?"

Flattered and pleased, I broke off a blossom to fasten in the lapel of his coat while Mama beamed with pleasure. All of my family pushed up next. We kissed and embraced, excited and thrilled. It hardly seemed possible that here we McCourts, all the way from Oshkosh, were about to sit down to supper with the great ones of the nation!

After the rest had congratulated us both, folding doors were opened by the servants and we moved into the next chamber to the supper table. The centerpiece was six feet high. A great basin of blossoms held a massive wedding bell of white roses, surmounted by a heart of red roses and pierced by an arrow of violets, shot from a Cupid's bow of heliotrope. At either end of the long table extending the whole length of the parlor, was a colossal four-leaf clover formed of red roses, white camelias and blue violets, garlanded with smilax.

Over a separate table required to support the wedding cake, was a canopy of flowers with trailing foliage. In each corner of the room was a bower of japonicas arranged in duplicate form to the boxes of the Tabor Grand Opera House at home in Denver. Violets encircled each guest's place at table and other flowers garlanded the champagne buckets.

"It's like fairyland—or heaven!" Mama whispered to me.

Supper was very gay. Everyone celebrated the occasion with hilarity and although President Arthur took his departure at about quarter to eleven, many of the other guests remained until midnight. It was a truly gala feast.

This was the first of March. With the next day, scandal broke in the papers. Father Chapelle returned the $200 wedding fee that Tabor had given him and publicly announced that he had been duped by Papa into marrying two divorced persons.

"When I asked the bride's father if he knew of any impediments to the marriage, he clearly answered he did not," Father Chapelle was quoted as explaining. "To say all in a few words, I was shamefully deceived by the McCourt family."

He also threatened to have the marriage declared illicit by carrying the question to the highest authorities in the Church. Eventually he thought better of it, after Tabor had sent Bill Brush around to pacify him. But Washington buzzed with gossip.

The next day a greater sensation occurred when the newspapers got hold of the fact that we had been secretly married six months previously in St. Louis and three months before Tabor's legal divorce from Augusta. Both Tabor and I publicly denied this because of the political prestige we hoped he would yet win.

"Just malice and envy of a great man," I told reporters.

The next day, Tabor's last day in the Senate, I went and sat in the ladies' gallery. I was dressed in one of my most stylish trousseau costumes, a brown silk dress with a tight-fitting bodice, and I wore a sparkling necklace, ear-rings and bracelets. I had on my jeweled waist-girdle in the shape of a serpent, with diamond eyes, ruby tongue and a long tail of emeralds. So attired I went to watch my husband during his final session. I could hear whispers going all around the assembly as I sought a seat and, pretty soon, masculine necks on the floor began to crane around in order to see me. I was the most talked-of figure in Washington. My beauty was discussed, my clothes, my jewels, my spectacular lover and husband, his lavish spending, all the details of our romance, and of

Augusta's position, our future plans and if the marriage would last—Washington and the nation talked of nothing else that week.

I suppose all of us frail mortals enjoy the limelight and I, as much as the next. Since only the flattering bits of conversations were repeated back to me, I was as proud as a peacock and immensely flattered by this wide-spread attention and admiration. Some of the papers were referring to me as the Silver Queen and none of them failed to speak of my blonde beauty. It was enough to turn the head of any twenty-eight-year-old (although, of course, I said I was twenty-two).

"I'm so happy I can't believe it's all true," I whispered to Tabor as we left Washington on a wedding tour to New York.

"But it's nothing to the happiness we're going to have," he answered, giving me an affectionate squeeze. "You'll be the first lady of Colorado next!"

When we returned to Denver, Tabor first settled me in a palatial suite at the Windsor Hotel. He gave a banquet to which he invited two hundred people. The liquor flowed until dawn and there were many speeches and toasts to Tabor and his greatness. Just before that, the Bavonne New Jersey *Statesman* had carried a banner headline reading "For President of the United States: Horace A. W. Tabor," and many people at the banquet referred to the article very seriously, complimenting us on the Senator's future.

"First lady of Colorado. Hell!" Tabor said. "You'll be first lady of the land!"

I shivered with excitement. It really seemed as if my wonderful husband would raise me to the most exalted height in the country. I, little Lizzie Mc-Court from Oshkosh!

But meanwhile, weeks began to drag by and no one came to see me. None of the ladies made party calls (which were absolutely obligatory in those days) and no one signified the least desire to welcome me as a newcomer to the ranks of Denver society. I wanted to succeed for myself. But even more, I wanted to succeed for Tabor as a helpmate. I wanted to be beside him in his brilliant career.

Tearfully, I broached the subject to Tabor.

"Don't worry, honey. It's just that they don't want to come to the hotel. Wait till we get settled in the home I've bought for you—then they'll be around."

Tabor first bought a fine house at 1647 Welton. It was brick with a verandah on the first floor and an awning-shaded porch on the second. But he wanted something more elaborate. In December, 1886, he found it.

The second house that Tabor bought was one of the most pretentious on Capitol Hill and cost $54,000. It was on Thirteenth Avenue and its grounds ran through from Sherman to Grant Avenue. A brown stone wall about three feet high ran around the lower end of the velvety lawn where the ground sloped down the hill, and it had two driveways to the stables. Tabor engaged five gardeners and housemen, two coachmen, and two footmen. We had three carriages and six horses.

Two pairs of horses were pure white. One carriage was brown trimmed in red. Another was dark blue enamel with thin gold striping, and lined with light blue satin. The last carriage was black, trimmed in white, and upholstered in white satin. I would order up the carriage and horses that best suited the costume I was wearing that day. Most often it was the blue carriage and the four glossy whites, caparisoned in shiny, brass-ornamented harness, to set off the blue of my eyes should anyone glance from the sidewalk to look at me.

Troops of children used to follow along behind my equipage every time the coach and footmen drove me downtown, exactly as if they were following a circus parade and would shout out comments on my color scheme of the day. Naturally the various uniforms of the servants matched the complete outfit planned around each dress. They were maroon for the brown carriage, blue for the blue, and black for the black, although I alternated and switched them for the most startling effect in relation to my own costume. One of the little girls who used to join the traipsing throng, later grew up to be one of Colorado's great women —Anne Evans (prime mover of the Central City Summer Festival).

But before the house was ready for occupancy, Tabor heard that General Sherman was to pay a visit to Leadville. He borrowed Dave Moffat's private car, loaded six cases of champagne aboard, and together we set out on the South Park line for the Clarendon Hotel.

"Well, this won't be like the time General Grant came to Leadville!" Tabor said with a happy sigh. And it wasn't.

Tabor met the famous Civil War general in the morning and escorted him on a tour of the mines. Later, in the evening, General Sherman and his party joined us at a special table set for us in the hotel while an orchestra, composed of miners that Tabor had engaged during the course of the day, played during dinner. Afterward we took the party to the Tabor Opera House. Our box was decorated in lilies—a custom Tabor always followed in both Leadville and Denver whenever I was to be in the audience—and throughout the performance, Tabor saw to it that the champagne corks kept popping.

General Sherman enjoyed himself immensely and in saying goodbye, bowed low over my hand with:

"The hospitality and beauty of the West amazes me."

Then he looked me directly in the eye, with a meaningful twinkle!

This was the second time that year that I had met men of national prominence, and on each occasion they had patently liked me. But why wouldn't their women accept me? I had done nothing really wrong. I hadn't stolen Tabor from Augusta, as they said. She had lost him first and then I had merely loved him more than she. I could hardly bear this turn of events.

Back in Denver, things were worse. Bill Bush and I had been growing more and more incompatible for a long time and I finally persuaded Tabor to bring on my younger brother, Peter McCourt, to have as his manager instead of Bill. This led to a very sensational public quarrel. Tabor brought suit against Bush for embezzling $2,000. Bush was acquitted and in reply, he placed a deposition before the Supreme Court, claiming that Tabor owed him $100,000 for various services rendered. He asked $10,000 for securing testimony and witnesses for Tabor's divorce at Durango, and for persuading Augusta at last to bring suit. He asked a larger sum for "—aiding him in effecting a marriage with the said Mrs. Doe, commonly called Baby Doe." He asked $1,547 for bribes paid to legislators during the Senatorial election, in sums ranging from $5 to $475, and the whole bill of particulars was equally dreadful. It was just a vile attack. (In truth, Bush owed Tabor; and Tabor later got judgment for $19,958.)

Luckily, the court struck the complaint from the record as indecent and irrelevant. But the harm had been done. Tabor's political prestige again waned. Tabor and Bush never made up this nasty quarrel, although Bush remained a friend and partner of young Maxcy Tabor, who had sided with Augusta at the time of the divorce. I had always distrusted Bush and now hated him.

"May the devil destroy his soul!" I used to say to Tabor.

Augusta and I met twice.

The first time was when I was living at the Windsor Hotel toward the end of 1881 and before I had moved to the American House. I was very surprised one afternoon to have the bellboy present a hand-written card on a salver. It read "Mrs. Augusta L. Tabor" and startled me so that I never found out what the "L" stood for—Augusta's maiden name was Pierce.

In December of 1880 Augusta had bought out Mr. Charles Hall's interest in the Windsor Hotel, and she had made a point of coming down and carefully going over the books with Bill Bush and Maxcy Tabor who was employed in the office. Personally, I had a feeling that she had done this not only to make a good investment but to keep a closer eye on Tabor's goings and comings. That particular day, he was away on business, and she undoubtedly knew it.

I had been reading a new novel by Georgia Craink and my thoughts were far away. I didn't want to receive Augusta but I knew it would only make more trouble if I didn't. So I told the bellboy to show Mrs. Tabor up.

It was one of the most uncomfortable interviews I ever had. Augusta kept sniffling about "Hod" (as she called Horace) and his disgusting taste in bad women. She talked about two of Horace's former mistresses—Alice Morgan, a woman who did a club-swinging act at the Grand Central in Leadville, and Willie Deville, a common prostitute, whom he had found in Lizzie Allen's parlor house in Chicago. Tabor had brought her back to Denver and set her up lavishly. Later, he had taken Willie on trips to St. Louis and New York, but terminated his affair with her by a gift of $5,000, claiming she talked too much.

"Why do you tell me these things?" I asked Augusta with as much steel as I could put into my voice. Inwardly, I was furious.

"To show you that if he tired of them, Hod's sure to tire of you."

"In that case, there's nothing more to say, Mrs. Tabor. I do not want your confidences."

Then she began to weep again and beg me to give her husband up. She blabbered in such a confused manner I could not possibly hear the exact words. I did not want to discuss Horace with her nor anyone else, and certainly not to talk about anything so intimate as our relationship. I had to think quickly.

"I will not give him up, Mrs. Tabor. If he chooses to give me up, then no doubt he will make me a parting gift, too. But I do not see that that concerns either of us. I have nothing more to say. Good-afternoon."

She left with her ramrod gait and, always after that call, her bitterness

56

and malice toward me were complete. Perhaps if I had been able to handle her more tactfully, she would not have been so obstinate about granting a divorce in the succeeding years. But I consider that she was very lucky that I didn't lose my Irish temper completely and throw things at her.

The second time was January 16, 1884, when Maxcy married Miss Luella Babcock. The occasion was formal and Augusta and I behaved accordingly. I was still a bride and the sensation of the nation. No one in the country was spending as much on their wardrobe as I was at that time. I had everything. Beauty, grace and charm were mine, as was a loving husband who lavished every conceivable extravagant attention on me. It seemed as if all doors were about to open for me.

But weeks and months dragged by and no women called. I might have felt this disappointment more poignantly if I hadn't been sustained by the happy knowledge that I was to have a baby in July. Tabor was as excited as a boy at the prospect, and was making all sorts of elaborate preparations for the most expensive layette a baby ever had. He planned a charmingly decorated nursery. The baby was to have every conceivable attention a doting father could arrange.

"I hope the baby is a girl," he would whisper to me fondly.

And the baby was a girl. She was born July 13, 1884, and we decided to take her to Oshkosh for her christening. Papa had died the year before, a couple of months after our marriage, and Mama would appreciate having us— and her granddaughter! Tabor was so ecstatic that he sent out to at least a hundred prominent citizens a small package containing a gold medallion the size of a twenty-five cent piece. On one side was inscribed

BABY TABOR
July 13
1884

On the obverse side was "Compliments of the Tabor Guards, Boulder, Colorado."

Employees of the Matchless mine sent her a gold-lined cup, saucer and spoon. It seemed as if the baby had been born to every luxury and joy. My own cup of bliss was overflowing for some time and I forgot all about the jealous cats and sanctimonious old battle-axes of Denver. I was a mother! The mother of an exquisite little girl. Tabor and I couldn't have been more proud.

For her christening, she had a real lace and hand-embroidered baby dress fastened with diamond-and-gold pins, special hand-made booties, and a tiny jeweled necklace with a diamond locket. The outfit cost over fifteen thousand dollars. Mama could not have been more elated when she saw the baby finally dressed and the name of Elizabeth Bonduel Lillie pronounced over her.

"Papa would have been so pleased to see you happy and settled down," she murmured several times.

For ten years this happiness lasted. There were minor heartaches along the stretch of that decade and some of these might have been major catastrophes if we had allowed ourselves to dwell on them. But we didn't. Tabor's investments spread like a network, everywhere, and the Matchless mine in Leadville continued to pour out its treasure of ore, often running as high as $80,000 a month. We had everything that money could buy.

But what I learned with hidden sadness in these years is that money doesn't buy everything. Tabor poured untold sums into the coffers of the Republican party in Colorado for which he never got the least consideration. He wanted the gubernatorial nomination. But consistently during the '80s, they took his money and denied him any recognition.

During this period two private sorrows came to me. One of them disturbed and vexed me for years. The other was a swift and desperate grief. The first unhappiness was because I made no real friends and had received no invitations in Denver. Through Tabor's prominence in Denver and Leadville, I met and entertained many men interested in politics. The famous beauties, Lily Langtry and Lillian Russell, and other well-known figures of the nineteenth century stage such as Sara Bernhardt, Mme. Modjeska, John Drew, Augustin Daly, William Gillette, Edwin Booth, and Otis Skinner frequently played at the Tabor Opera House, and Tabor and I would entertain them at champagne suppers after their performances. They always seemed to like me and would ask to see me on our fairly frequent visits to New York. The excitement of these friendships, knowing the great artists of my day, proved a great compensation for my early ambition to go on the stage. But the society women of Denver remained steadfastly aloof.

The other sorrow was the loss of my baby son. He was born October 17, 1888, and lived only a few hours. I suppose every mother wants a boy, and this new chastisement from God made my life almost unbearable. I had no real place in life except as a good wife and mother and I wanted for Tabor's sake to be able to fulfill this place to my very best. Augusta had borne him a son and I wanted to, too. I cried silently in the nights about his death, longing for another boy.

But this was not to be. On December 17, 1889, I had another daughter, Rose Mary Echo Silver Dollar Tabor, whom I nicknamed "Honeymaid." But most of her friends as she grew up called her Silver. Lillie, the first little girl, was blonde like myself, but Silver was dark like Tabor, and very lovely in appearance.

By the time she was born, many of Tabor's mines had fallen off in output, but the Matchless was still bearing up. Some of Tabor's other investments had not turned out as we thought, although we were still hopeful and felt it was just a question of time. We continued to live on the same lavish scale; Tabor mortgaged the Tabor Block and the Opera House until some of the other mines he had bought should begin to pay.

Silver had nearly as gorgeous clothes and toys and ponies as Lillie did. But this was not to be for long. However, at that time we had no inkling of what the future held for us. Tabor made frequent business trips East and to his mining properties. Mostly I went with him but sometimes I stayed with the children. His holdings were enormous and he was expanding in many directions that required his personal attention. He bought a yacht in New York

City with the idea that when the children were older we would cruise down to Honduras to see his mahogany forests.

Peter McCourt, my bachelor brother, meanwhile was fast making himself a secure place in Denver both in the social world and in financial circles. Since everything he had was due to me, it was particularly galling that he should be asked everywhere that I was barred.

One night he was entertaining a group of his friends at poker in our house. Will Macon, Jack Moseby, Will Townsend, John Kerr and John Good, all from good families, were there. After the game was over he planned to serve them an elaborate champagne supper which our servants were in the habit of preparing whenever Tabor and I entertained.

I was upstairs alone. Tabor was away on one of his business trips. I got to brooding about how unfair everyone in Denver had been both to him and me. They had punished him politically for nothing else than that he had fallen in love with another woman, and they had cruelly ignored me, making me suffer over and over again for having given myself to the man I loved before we were married. No one gave me credit for being a tender mother and faithful wife. They merely stared at me with their noses in the air.

But stare, they did. When I would attend the theatre and sit in Box A (which Tabor had had re-upholstered in white satin), they would raise their opera glasses or lorgnettes to study every detail of my costume. Then they would go away and have their own cheap dressmakers copy my designs. My clothes and hats were good enough to imitate, but I was not good enough to be received!

The more I thought about this, the more furious I grew. I jumped to my feet and began to pace up and down the floor.

"It's all so unjust," I thought to myself. "The very mothers and sisters of those bachelors downstairs are making me pay today for something I did long ago. I didn't hurt Augusta—why should they hurt me?"

As I paced, my temper mounted. Finally, in a burst of rage, I ran down the large oak stairs and into the dining room where the young men were seated at table, laughing and talking. I stamped my foot.

"If I'm not good enough for your mothers and sisters to call on, how can my food be good enough for you to eat?" I demanded at the top of my voice. My hands trembled with the fury their easy-going faces aroused in my breast.

Pete looked up at me, startled at my behavior. It was hardly news, my not being accepted. The situation had gone on for years. The expression on his face only infuriated me further. I stamped my foot again.

"Go on and get out!" I shrieked. "If your women haven't got enough manners to call on me, I don't want you around here eating my food and drinking my wine."

The boys had risen at my sudden entrance. Now, embarrassed by my attack, they began to put down the morsels of food they still had in their hands. With heads down, they began shuffling from the room.

"Well, good night, Pete," they mumbled.

After the door had closed on their unceremonius departure, Pete turned on me:

"What do you mean by saying I could have my friends over and then causing a scene like this. Do you want to disgrace me?"

"Disgrace you! Everything you have in the world is due to Tabor and me. If you had any gratitude, you'd have your friends invite me to their parties—not use me to further your own ends!"

This led to a violent argument and we did not speak for several days. Eventually, Pete and I talked this all out and we made up our differences. We were very close, as he was just two years younger than I. But the day was to come, when we were to part forever. I never forgave him for not helping Tabor in his hour of need. Of that, more later.

I didn't always lose my temper, however, over these slights. Sometimes I maintained a real sense of humor. One day one of the coachmen came to me and said:

"If you please, ma'am, the maid next door says that one of the reasons the ladies don't call is because of all those naked figures on the lawn. They think they're indecent."

I thanked him with a twinkle in my eye.

"How absolutely silly!" I thought.

The figures that stood on our lawn were the very finest masterpieces cast by the same Parisian bronze foundry that cast the sculpture of Rodin. They had been especially ordered and shipped from Europe. There were two sweet little deer that stood by the carriage entrance in front, and in the corners by the shrubs were Psyche, Nimrod, and Diana, of Grecian gracefulness. Perhaps these figures were somewhat advanced for a town that had been a frontier only a few years before, but they certainly weren't indecent.

I sent the coachman down to fetch the costumer and when he arrived, I commanded:

"Now make me clothes exactly to fit these figures. I want Nimrod with red hunting boots and a derby hat. I want Diana in flowing chiffon and panties underneath, and I want Psyche in stiff satin."

He surveyed me as if I were crazy.

"The maid next door says her mistress can't stand these naked figures—they shock her," I explained. "These clothes are for the neighbor's benefit, not mine."

The costumer did as he was bid and in a couple of weeks, my statues were all fitted out to the Queen's taste—Queen Victoria's. But underneath the banter of my attitude and the humor of my little stunt, there was a heart that was sore. My husband couldn't rise as he should and my children were excluded from the normal place they should hold, because I and my former actions were frowned on. Any wife and mother must know how deeply worried I was behind my pertness and bravery.

Yet suddenly all this didn't matter. Real tragedy fell on us. The year 1893 arrived and with it the silver panic. Almost overnight, we who had been the richest people in Colorado were the poorest. It seems incredible that it should have all happened so quickly, but with one stroke of President Cleveland's pen, establishing the demonetization of silver, all of our mines, and particularly the Matchless, were worthless.

Tabor's other holdings which had sounded so spectacular and so promising on paper, turned out, many of them, to be literally paper. He had been duped or cheated by associates and friends for years without either of us realizing it. Some of his real estate was already mortgaged, and, when the blow first fell, he mortgaged the rest. Afterward we learned what a mistake that was. We should have learned to economize immediately.

But none of the mining men believed the hard times would last. Ten Denver banks failed in three days during July and our cash went when they crashed. Gradually, with no money coming in, we could not meet payments on the mortgages. The banks wouldn't loan us any more money and our property began to fall on the foreclosure block.

"Take my jewels and sell them, Tabor," I volunteered.

"No, the day will come when you'll wear them again. I'll make another fortune. That gold mine I bought near Ward and never developed will help us out. The world wants gold now—not silver."

Before the house was taken from us, the Tabor Block in Denver and all the Leadville properties fell. What wasn't taken for mortgages, began to go for unpaid taxes. When I had married Tabor, he had spent $10,000 a day during his thirty-day stay in Washington because at that time his income from the Matchless alone had been $80,000 a month. Yet just ten years after, we were actually worried about our grocery bill.

I knew Tabor's dearest possession, next to the Matchless mine, was the Tabor Grand Opera House. When the mortgage owners gave notice of foreclosure on that, I went personally to plead with young Horace Bennett for an extension of time and leniency.

"We millionaires must all stick together," I said.

He regarded me with cold blue eyes and replied:

"I am not a millionaire, Mrs. Tabor, and this is a business transaction. I appreciate how you and Mr. Tabor have sentimental feelings about the Opera House. But in that case, you shouldn't have mortgaged it."

I could not make him share my belief that Tabor would recoup everything. In my innermost heart, I knew he would. But here was a new kind of man in Colorado who did not look at life the way the first-comers did. Those men were plungers, gay and generous. When they had money, they spent it and when they didn't, they had the bravery to start out on new ventures and make other fortunes. When a friend was down, they loaned him more than he needed and forgot the loan. That was Tabor. But not these newcomers who were settling and growing prosperous in Colorado.

And even my own brother! I went to Pete to save the Opera House for Tabor.

"I haven't the money, and even if I had, you'd only mortgage it over again for some silly extravagance," he said.

I was furious. From that day until he died in 1929 I never forgave him. When his will was read, he had left a quarter of a million dollars but he only left me, who had made all his affluence possible, some worthless carriage stock. He was the most bitter disappointment of my life.

There was one man who was an exception. He was W. S. Stratton of

Colorado Springs who made many millions in the Independence mine in Cripple Creek. When he heard of Tabor's plight, he wrote him a check for $15,000 to use in developing his Eclipse mine in Boulder County.

"There's a true friend," Tabor remarked with touching humility. It wrung me to the quick to see him act like this, pathetic and almost beaten. When he had had money, and even in the days before I knew him and before he became rich, his generosity and honesty had been proverbial. In return, the·world gave him only deceit and niggardliness—and a cold shoulder. Many a night I wept with secret rage at the world as much as sorrow for Tabor.

Once again I openly lost my temper. Workmen came to our house to turn off the lights and water because of unpaid bills. Tabor protested against this humiliation but without success. Finally he turned back into the house saying:

"Well, tell your bosses how I feel about it."

Gathering up my skirts, I flew into the yard like a wildcat.

"The idea of your doing this to Tabor! The man who gave Denver its beautiful Opera House! The man who has done much more for this town than ever it deserved. He's invested large sums in your very own business and helped most of your own officers to political positions. Why, this is an outrage!"

"Orders is orders," they replied belligerently, and went on with their work.

"Well, just wait until Congress changes that ridiculous law about silver and the Matchless is running again! Then you'll be sorry you acted like this."

I had lived all my grown-up life with miners. I could not believe, even if the rich vein of our fortune had thinned, that the pay ore would not widen again a little further on. I had implicit faith in my husband and his judgment. I have always had implicit faith in the Matchless. But sometimes it has been hard to make others understand.

When I had no visible effect on these men, I turned to Tabor and said: "Well, lets make a game of it."

So we giggled while we carried lighted candles from room to room of the great house, and toted our drinking water from a barrel—water hauled to the house from the Old Courthouse pump. Somehow I kept our spirits up. Whenever Tabor was around, it was a game—I insisted on it for his benefit. But soon the illusion was gone. No game was possible when the Eclipse mine proved worthless.

The house was foreclosed. We lived in cheap little rooms in West Denver. I did all the cooking, washing, ironing and sewing. I worked early in the morning and late at night to make Tabor presentable to appear downtown with his business associates, and to have Lillie look nice when she went to school. During those bleak years of the mid '90s, our affairs went consistently from bad to worse. My jewels, except a few choice pieces, were pawned or sold for necessities. Some times we didn't have enough to eat. But I carried my head high, knowing that Tabor luck was sure and that our fortunes were bound to change.

Tabor was past sixty-five and suddenly he was an old man. He worked as an ordinary laborer in Leadville, wheeling slag at the smelter. But he was not up to the strenuous physical effort. And the pay was only $3.00 a day. At the other end of town, the Matchless was shut down and her shafts and drifts were fast filling with water after the stopping of the pumps.

Desperation haunted our every move. I could not believe that what I had laughingly spent for one of the children's trinkets just a few years ago would now keep the whole family in groceries for a month. During this gloomy period, which lasted for five years, my greatest consolation was Silver. She was four years old when the catastrophies first began to fall and had no realization of what was happening. But her disposition was always sweet and hopeful. She was a laughing, affectionate child, and adored both her father and me.

"Darling, darling Silver" I would murmur, tucking her into bed beside her sister. "What would I ever do without you?"

When it seemed that none of us could survive the strain any longer and that really all hope was lost, Senator Ed Wolcott whom I had met in Central City and who had been both a former friend and a political enemy of Tabor's in Leadville and in Denver, came to the rescue. Through his intercession, he succeeded in getting President McKinley to appoint Tabor postmaster of Denver.

"Our luck is back!" I cried, clapping my hands in glee. "It was when you were postmaster of Leadville that you struck it rich. I'm sure this is a sign. Pretty soon, you'll have it all back!"

We moved into a simple two-room suite, No. 302, in the Windsor Hotel. It was on the corner above the alley, but with an uplifting view of the mountains. Tabor went to work for the government. He was very grateful and pleased with his position, although I thought much more should have been done for him. Still, he enjoyed the work, and the regular routine of his job. He settled down into being a quiet wage-earner and family man. He practiced petty economies to live on $3,500 a year, a sum he had lost many times on one hand of poker. Now his luncheon was a sandwich at his desk. But he loved me and the children and he seemed to be really content, despite the modesty of our circumstances.

"But you will be the great Tabor again," I insisted from time to time. I felt very deeply that his present simple occupation was too mean for the great builder and benefactor that Tabor had been, a deplorable way to end his days! It simply could not be.

He would pat my hand and say:

"My dear, brave little Baby. So trusting, so constant, so hard-working—and always so cheerful! Your love has been the most beautiful thing in my life."

I cherished this tribute tenderly and have often thought of it in the years since. The snobbish society women of Denver had been sure I would leave Tabor the moment his fortune collapsed. I suppose if I had ever really been what they thought me, I would have—but they had never given me credit for the sincerity of my love. When the crash came, I was thirty-eight years old. My beauty had hardly diminished at all. Several men sought me out to make clandestine overtures when I was alone in the cheap rooms in West Denver. But I sealed the knowledge of their visits and who these men were—one of them had been, some years before, a supposedly good friend of Tabor's. My pride was incensed by their offers.

"What sort of a wife do you think I am?" I demanded indignantly, and sent them unceremoniously on their way.

But now the year was 1899. Tabor had held his job only a year and three months in April, when he was taken violently ill with appendicitis. I called in three doctors for advice. They mentioned an operation but were doubtful of the outcome because of Tabor's advanced age. Tabor had always had a marvelous constitution and I felt sure he would pull through without an operation. Besides, I was afraid of surgery.

For seven days and nights, I nursed him. I was by his bedside constantly, never letting myself sleep except in cat-naps during this long vigil. Often he was in too great pain to speak. Occasionally, the suffering would let up, and we would talk a little.

"Never let the Matchless go, if I die, Baby," he said once. "It will make millions again when silver comes back."

The week dragged endlessly by while worry and strain bore me down with fatigue. Had I made the right decision? Would Tabor recover?

On the morning of April 10, the doctors who had come to examine Tabor, led me gently aside and told me the end was near. Nervous and weak from loss of sleep and doubt about the decision I had made regarding the operation, I collapsed. It was not until the afternoon that I knew anything, because drugs had been administered to me, and I had been taken into another bedroom. When I came to, the nurse said:

"Your husband has gone."

"Tabor, dead! Never!" I cried.

I tried all afternoon not to believe what they said, but finally I could deny the truth no longer. Desperate grief weighed me down oppressively. I was forty-four years old and my great love affair was over. Never would I have any further life. What was I to do?

And almost as if the angels above had heard my harassed question, I heard Tabor's words ringing in my ears:

"Hang on to the Matchless. It will make millions again."

Chapter Five

Fortunately for my state of mind, Tabor's death was received with the prestige due a great man. I think that if his passing had been snubbed as he himself had been in his last years, I could not have borne my sorrow. But his going was solemnized as it should have been.

"Deepest condolences to the widow of Senator Tabor," arrived from the governor of Colorado, the mayor of Denver, the legislature, the city council and every civic and fraternal order in the state. Flowers filled our hotel suite to overflowing. Telegrams arrived in bundles from all over the country. It was a magnificent tribute.

"Oh, Silver! Oh, Lillie!" I cried between my tears and smiles, "Papa would be so happy if he could but know!"

Flags were ordered at half mast on federal, state and city buildings. The body was taken to the Capitol and viewed by thousands. At night the doors were closed and four soldiers of the state militia stood guard over the catafalque in the governor's room. Floral pieces of many designs were sent by the hundreds to the Capitol as well as to us. A list of these donors filled more than a column in the newspapers. Leadville sent a floral piece of roses six feet high and four feet wide, designed like a cornucopia to symbolize the Tabor Plenty.

"He would be most pleased with that gift," I explained to the girls. "Papa really loved Leadville."

At the funeral, services were first held in the Capitol. Then there was a parade of federal and state soldiers, police and firemen. Four bands marched in the procession. The cortege filed slowly along Broadway and turned down Seventeenth St., finally making its way to Sacred Heart Church at Twenty-eighth and Larimer Sts. Four priests officiated at the church rites, Father Berry making the principal address.

Ten thousand people gathered along the line of march and as I peered out from under my heavy black veil, I wanted to throw a kiss to each and every one of them.

"Papa was a truly great man—they have come because they know that," I whispered to the girls who were riding in the same carriage with me. And from somewhere, there began to run through my head the line: "In death a hero, as in life a friend."

I had been weeping off and on for days and this thought brought on a fresh gust of racking sobs. It seemed as if I just could never regain control of myself! I was spent with grief.

The parade re-formed after the church service and made its final march to Calvary cemetery, a Catholic plot, beyond present ₄Cheesman Park. Brief services followed at the grave side where we had gathered in a knot about the coffin.

"Oh, Mama, Mama, Mama, don't let them put Papa down there!" Silver suddenly shrieked when she saw the body being lowered into the ground. Silver and Lillie, both became hysterical and had to be led away to a carriage by the members of my family who were with me. But the girls' hysteria was contagious. In a burst of sobs, I rushed to the casket and threw myself on its floral covering, possessed by some mad notion of being buried with Tabor.

"There, there, Mrs. Tabor, you're overwrought," the priest soothed while several people lifted me off. I was calmer as the men began to shovel in the dirt and finally when the gathering began to disperse and move off toward the carriages, I mustered enough voice to say:

"Please leave me alone here. Tell my coachman to wait at the gateway. I will come a little later."

Actually I sat and knelt there for hours. Evening came and the cold April stars commenced to twinkle in the sky. I prayed and prayed, mostly incoherent desires, but frequently that Tabor and I should be re-united in heaven not too long away and I should have strength to carry on alone. I prayed a little for Tabor, too, but not much. I knew that so good and generous a man as he really was, despite some of his minor transgressions, must surely find a safe, restful haven in the Lord's eyes. He would be happier than we.

My premonition was all too true. Happiness was his reward but not ours.

For about two years, we struggled on in Denver, trying to eke out a living. Every hour I could take from housework, I spent in an endeavour to secure capital for re-possessing and improving the Matchless and made many calls on bankers and business men up and down 17th St. During the twenty-five years since my arrival as the bride of Harvey Doe, Denver had grown into the metropolis of the Rocky Mountains region. By 1901, the town was known as the "Queen City of the Plains" and had a population of 150,000, a phenomenal growth from the 30,000 of the pioneer community I had first seen. In this more urban atmosphere, investors were not drawn to mining the way they had been formerly—they were turning to reclamation projects, sugar beet factories and tourist attractions.

Lillie was a grown girl by now and Silver was just entering adolescence. They were both lovely looking but Silver was much more the child of Tabor's and my great love. Lillie was silent and distant and each year that she grew older, more contemptuous of my ideas.

"It's all rot there being any millions in that hole in the ground," Lillie frequently remarked. "Why, that mine was completely worked out years ago."

Such disdain was treason to Silver and me. Our adored Tabor had said it would bring us millions again as soon as silver came back and we believed him implicitly. I kept on with my efforts, and persistence finally told. Claudia McCourt, the one sister who had remained loyal to me, bought back the Matchless at a sheriff's sale in July, 1901. Oh, what a wonderful lucky day that seemed! I knew that Tabor would be proved right and I hurried home to tell the girls.

"We'll move up to Leadville and be right there on the ground to see that they don't cheat us or steal any ore. Tabor always said to beware of 'high-graders.' You girls will love spending the summer in the mountains."

Silver was thrilled at the prospect and entered into my plans with ardent enthusiasm. Lillie was very dubious about the whole project, both opening the mine and living in Leadville. But when the day came for us to move, she boarded the train with no further comment. We took rooms at 303 Harrison Avenue (the very building where Jake Sands had first lived—but all that seemed to me now as if it had never been!) and settled down to become residents of Leadville.

Silver soon made many friends and entered into the youngsters' life in Leadville with a vim. She had a natural sweetness and warmth like her father's that attracted people to her immediately. But Lillie spent most of her time writing letters to her friends in Denver, shut up in a room away from us.

"Come," I said to them one day when we had driven out on Fryer Hill close to the mine. "You must put on overalls and go down the shaft into the Matchless the way I do so that when you inherit this bonanza, you'll know all about it."

Silver was elated at the idea and rushed into the hoist house to look for miner's work clothes. But Lillie was rebellious.

66

"Then I'm going to run away!"

Later she secretly arranged for money from her uncle, Peter McCourt in Denver, for train fare back to Chicago, Illinois, to live with the McCourt relatives there. After Tabor had settled a substantial sum on Mama and Papa, at the time of my marriage, I thought my older sisters should have stayed loyal to me. But when Pete and I broke, they sided with Pete, although Mama tried to gloss matters over. Soon after, Mama died and the break was open.

For my own daughter to desert and go with those traitors to me—it was unthinkable! I was crushed.

Yet so it was that Lillie passed from my life.

After that ugly, unfortunate day, I seldom mentioned her name to anyone and she rarely communicated with me. It was almost as if I had never borne her as my baby nor exhibited her with such pride. Those many matinees when I had carried her in my arms through the foyer of the Tabor or taken her riding beside me in our handsome carriage on the streets of Denver so that all should see my darling first-born, had vanished completely.

My beautiful fair-haired baby with her exquisite clothes was no more; those days were like a dream that had passed. The first nine years of her adoring mother's lavish attention and the later ten years of grueling, slaving work to keep her clothed and fed, had alike fallen away and were as if they had never been. My last sight of her was as she piled her belongings in the back of a hired buggy and drove off to the railroad station.

"Oh, how cruel, how cruel life has been to me!" I moaned as the buggy pulled away. Closing the door, I started on foot up town, hardly conscious that I wanted to be able to pray alone in the Church of the Annunciation on Seventh Street. Lillie's buggy was disappearing and now I needed the strength of prayer and the reassurance of the Virgin's beatific smile.

As I knelt alone in the white interior praying ardently, I gazed heavenward at the imitation frescoes, replicas of classics pasted to the wall. Slowly courage returned to me. I must still carry on—for Tabor's name and for Silver's future. That thought came to me stronger and stronger, bathed in the white light of a real revelation. Gradually the almost trance-like state, that I must have been in for a long time, subsided and I came back to the sharp realities of life.

"I wonder who all those saints are?" I mused to myself, again glancing at the ceiling as I rose to go. I knew very little about spiritual matters except for occasional readings in the Bible and I determined I should know more. So before trudging the mile and a half home, I headed for the library.

"This will be what you want, I think," the very nice girl said in answer to my query, and handed me "The Lives of the Saints." From that day on, it was my favorite book. I read and re-read it throughout the years, supplementing its message with daily chapters from the Bible.

Meanwhile Silver was my pride and joy. When I got back to our house,

I told her about Lillie's abrupt departure, trying to remain calm and self-controlled as I narrated the episode.

"Good riddance to bad rubbish!" Silver answered impudently and threw her arms around my neck. "Don't let her hurt your feelings, Mama. She'll be sorry. When I'm a great authoress and you're a rich society woman in Denver, she'll come running back. Then she'll think differently about the Tabor name."

For some time Silver had had an ambition to write and was already contributing extra poems to her English work in eighth grade. Now I hugged her gratefully for her sympathy about Lillie and her encouragement for the future. She had her father's coloring and much of his character. How proud he would have been of her if he could have seen her at that moment!

"Yes, yes, I'm sure you're right, Silver. Lillie will be sorry and come back— and with your talent, you will make the Tabor name once again a thing of lustre!"

Slow and silent, in some ways, and quickly and noisily in others, the years slipped away. I had mortgaged the Matchless again, for development work, with the expectation that when the shaft was sunk to a slightly lower level, we would strike high-grade ore. But I was never able to lease the mine to the right group of men to carry out my idea.

"Nobody knows anything about mining any more!" I would cry with exasperation. "All the real miners like Tabor are dead."

Through their ignorance and bad management, the mine ate up capital. Although the leases paid occasionally in rent and royalties, those sums were only large enough to keep Silver and me supplied with adequate clothing and food. For a while, we rented a small house in town, once on Seventh St. and at another period, on Tenth St. But the Matchless never paid profits sufficient enough to dispell the mortgage. Once more, foreclosure hung over our heads.

"Silver," I said as we sat down to dinner. "We must go down to Denver and open my safety box. Papa wouldn't let me sell the very last of my jewels— but now, we must. I'm sure he would understand. The Matchless must be saved. Those were his last words."

"Oh, Mama! Your beautiful jewelry!"

"Oh, well, I don't have any use for it now. And when the Matchless pays again, I can buy more."

Silver and I frequently journeyed to Denver on pleasure trips or jauntily to pass some of the long cold winters when the mine had to be shut down. But this trip was a sad occasion. It was no easy matter to part with those treasures, given to me by my dearly loved husband. But I was determined they should go. I must keep a stiff upper lip. At the bank, Silver cried:

"Oh, not your engagement ring—and not Papa's watch-fob!"

My engagement ring was a single pure diamond, an enormous stone, surrounded by sapphires and set in gold which Tabor had panned himself in his early days at California Gulch. His watch-fob was a massive piece of gold artwork presented to him by the citizens of Denver on the opening night of the Tabor Grand Opera House. Three engraved pictures in ornament, The Tabor Grand Opera House, the Tabor Block in Denver and the Tabor Store in Oro in

California Gulch, were suspended in links from a triangle of gold held by a closed fist. On either side of the richly carved medallions ran mine ladders of gold down to a lacy array of miner's tools below the medallions. These, in turn, held a bucket of golden quartz, filled with gold and silver nuggets. On the reverse side, were monograms in fine enamel and the legend "Presented by the citizens of Denver to H. A. W. Tabor," and "Labor Omnia Vincet."

"That must be our talisman, Mama," Silver suggested. "We must never part with that."

I felt in my bones Silver was right and I ordered those two pieces put back into the safety deposit box. But the rest of the jewelry went to pay debts just as the diamonds of Queen Isabella of Spain had previously. My wedding present! What a sad memory! I never could bear to go back to that vault—I was afraid I should burst into tears. But Silver returned in 1911 and brought the two pieces to me at about the time we decided to make our permanent home in Leadville, living at the Matchless cabin to save rent.

"I met Mr. Edgar McMechen coming out and I showed him Papa's fob," she told me. "He thought it was gorgeous and said to be careful of that—that it was of great historical interest. I told him I wanted you to see it again—that you needed cheering up—and just to see it, would help you from getting discouraged and blue."

"You are a sweet, thoughtful daughter," I answered, kissing her. "I will look at them for inspiration. Then I will give them to the sisters at St. Vincent's hospital in Leadville. They are always so kind to us and will store anything I ask."

But it was the year before that, in 1910, that Silver had given me my greatest happiness about her. In 1908, President Roosevelt had visited Leadville and Silver had ridden into town to see him. That evening when she came back to the cabin, she wrote a lyric entitled "Our President Roosevelt's Colorado Hunt." A. S. Lohmann of Denver later set it to music and we had it published. The *Denver Post* wrote up her accomplishment and printed a picture of Silver two columns wide. I was so pleased!

Two years later President Roosevelt, although no longer in office, returned to Colorado and made an address in Denver. Silver was there, close to the platform, and when the speech was ended, was presented to him as the author of the Roosevelt song. The ex-president willingly posed with my daughter and the next day, the Denver newspapers printed photographs of Silver and President Roosevelt shaking hands.

"My darling, brilliant daughter!" I exclaimed in natural maternal pride when I saw the account. "Again a Tabor associates with a president of the United States—the Tabor luck is coming back!"

But I was wrong—that was the last day I was to experience great joy. My dearest treasure, Silver, with her piquant profile and sweet demure ways, was marked already with the shadow of tragedy. She had grown up very fond of horses and riding. I could not afford anything for her to ride but a burro that I used for hauling out ore from the mine. She used to hang around the livery stable hoping for better things.

One of the partners was a big man who always wore an enormous white ten-gallon hat and looked like a Western sheriff. He was a picturesque figure in a common way. Generously, he fell into the habit of loaning Silver riding horses, especially a spirited seventeen-hand cream gelding which would carry her thundering up Harrison Avenue with a speed to delight her romantic fancy. It was natural that she should be grateful and linger after the ride, talking horseflesh in a friendly way.

Nothing untoward about this arrangement occurred to me since the man was old enough to be a responsible citizen. He had known her from the time she was a little girl trudging up and down Little Stray Horse Gulch with a gunny sack over her shoulder, hauling mail and supplies. All the old-timers made it a point to be kind to her—like Big Jim McDonald who was running the Monarch mine up above us and frequently gave her a lift in his buggy, or like Henry Butler, editor of the *Herald-Democrat,* who loaned her a typewriter and helped her with her writing. I was not even suspicious until it was too late.

When the village gossip reached my ears, I fell into a soft moaning but then quickly denied the idea to my informant as impossible. But when I was by myself, I moaned aloud.

For years, my fond hopes had built such castles-in-Spain for Silver—with her dark prettiness and her unusual talent, no future could be too roseate for her—and now I was beside myself with worry. The Matchless had been mortgaged again, this time for $9,000 with an interest rate of 8%, and I was having more trouble with the lessees. There was no money with which to send Silver away.

"What course should I take?" I asked myself in desperation.

Before I could come to any decision, matters gathered to a drastic head. A few nights later, Silver set off for an Easter Monday ball in a lovely silk dress I had made her and a fur-trimmed coat (since at 10,000 feet altitude the spring nights are like icy winter). The party was to be given for the nice young people of the town. She went with two boys who were sons of substantial Leadville families.

But when Silver came in, it was eight-o-clock in the morning and she was drunk. Her dress was disheveled and she had no coat. The lovely blue silk dress was torn and dirty. And she was alone!

"Silver, what on earth has happened?" I cried. But she was too incoherent for me to make head or tail of her story. Fearful that she would catch pneumonia from exposure, I stirred up the fire in the stove and got the temperature of the cabin to the perspiring point. I put her to bed and she was soon sleeping it off.

But when I went to town for the mail, the news was all over town—a sordid story involving a saloon keeper. In a flash, my mind was made up.

"Write to your Uncle Peter," I said that evening at supper, "and ask him for enough money for you to go to Denver and get a job on a newspaper. There's no opportunity for your talent in this town and no chance to meet a man really worthy of you."

I was much too proud to appeal to Pete, myself, after our quarrel, but on several occasions I had permitted Silver to do so. In justice to Pete, I must admit he always responded—and I always felt he was trying to make up for the way he acted at the time of Tabor's collapse.

Silver left for Denver shortly after. For a while, she made good as a reporter on the *Denver Times*, and, later, in Chicago she wrote a novel, "Star of Blood." But good fortune did not last. When she was out of money and a job, she wrote to me in Leadville.

"Mama," she mused on paper, "I think I will enter a convent. You have always been very religious and I am turning in that direction more and more—perhaps that would be a fine solution for my life."

I had always pictured Silver with a dazzling, high place before the world. But when I realized how the world was changing her from the sweet, pretty little girl she had been to a woman, bruised and at the mercy of men's lust, I welcomed the thought of the serenity and spiritual safety of a convent. I was giving up my life to the Matchless. It was fitting that my daughter should give up her life to her God. They were both dedications to a love higher than self.

"If you don't hear from me," she went on, "you will know that I can't write—that I've taken vows."

My breath choked in my throat. I had lost everything—everything in the world that I prized—my dear husband, money, prominence, all my fineries, jewelry and the many little luxuries a woman loves, my brother, my family, my first daughter—and now Silver! It was almost more than one heart could stand. I cried out in terror.

"Oh, no, Silver! I can't lose you."

Little by little, I became reconciled to her suggestion. My darling baby was going away—but she was not really going away. She would be with me always.

Shortly after that, she managed to raise enough capital to start and edit a little paper called the "Silver Dollar Weekly." But after a few issues, its financial success was too negligible to carry on. Her letters said she was giving the project up and going to Chicago. If she failed there she would enter a convent in the mid-West that Uncle Peter knew about.

The years passed slowly by. A few letters came and then only silence. Imagine my horror one September night in 1925! I had come to Denver to pass the winter and had stopped at the desk of my cheap little hotel before going to bed. The clerk surveyed me with a kind of contemptuous awe and asked:

"Is that your daughter I seen in the paper tonight was murdered in some Chicago scandal?"

"Certainly not," I flared back. "My daughter is in a convent."

I could not afford to buy a newspaper so I hurried to the Denver Public Library in the Civic Center. What could the story be? Perhaps the clerk meant Lillie—I never mentioned her name nor even admitted she was my daughter—but something might have happened to her or her husband that revealed who she really was. As I clumped into the library, dressed, as usual, in my black dress, veiled motoring cap headgear and heavy boots, the clock said a few minutes past nine-thirty.

71

"Oh, dear," I said to the librarian at the desk. "Am I too late to read tonight's paper? I know the newspaper files close at half-past nine—"

She looked up and with some penetration, perhaps recognition, gazed at me for a brief instant.

"Yes, the newspaper room is closed. But if you will go in and sit down in the reference room, I think I can manage to bring you an evening paper."

I thanked her very pleasantly and did as she bade. While I waited, I absently traced the grain of the heavy walnut with my finger nail, trying not to show any distress. Soon she quietly laid the paper down in front of me and stole away. But with that sixth sense you have in a crisis, out of the back of my head I could feel the librarians watching me.

"Silver!" I gasped to myself and wanted to faint.

But I made myself sit extremely straight and read very quietly, knowing there were alien eyes observing me. The account told of a young woman, who had posed under various aliases but lastly as Ruth Norman. She had been scalded to death under very suspicious circumstances in a rooming house in the cheapest district in Chicago. She was a perpetual drunk, was addicted to dope and had lived with many men of the lowest order. But her doctor knew who she really was. She was Rose Mary Echo Silver Dollar Tabor, who had signed her songs Silver Echo Tabor and her novel, Rose Tabor.

"My darling little Honeymaid!" I wailed inwardly and thought my heart must break. My eyes blurred with tears so that I could not read. "What a ghastly tragic end—poor, poor little girl!"

A strange photograph had been found in her room on which Silver had written this warning: "In case I am killed, arrest this man." He was later identified as a saloon-keeper who had been one of her lovers. But insufficient evidence was brought out at the coroner's inquest to attach definite guilt to him.

To save Silver's body from the potter's field, Peter McCourt was wiring $200 for the burial of his niece.

"Damn him!" was my thought. He seemed always, at every blow my life sustained, to be in a position to make my humiliation more soul-searing.

Deliberately I read the whole account through a second time. I knew with profound conviction that every line was true—I could piece together the whole story step by step. But following that awful downfall, there under the white-bowled lights of the library, my conscience cried out that I had failed again—failed, as a mother, more miserably than ever Augusta could have wished or prophesied. I was bowed down with shame.

"Don't let anyone know," my heart immediately rebelled. "The Tabor pride does not admit defeat."

Gathering up the paper quietly and folding its pink sheets along their original creases, I took it to the desk and nonchalantly handed the death-blow back to the girl who had brought it to me.

72

"Thank you very much for the paper," I said. "But that story's all a pack of lies. She's not my daughter—that young woman. I *know* Silver is in a convent."

Turning on my heel, I walked out, erect and dignified, my miner's boots clacking with the conviction of my statement.

So passed Silver from my life. I don't know which was sadder or more humiliating—Silver's going or Lillie's. From the viewpoint of the world, I suppose it was Lillie's. But from my own, I was devoted to Silver and believed in her, and her going was the hardest to bear. I knew she had told me the lie about the convent to protect me from hurt. But in the end, the hurt was much greater.

I have never admitted my hurt, even to intimates. Before the world, I have always preserved the outline of her fabrication. Silver is alive today. She is in a convent.

The winter dragged miserably in and I was even poorer. My boots wore out and I hit upon the scheme of wrapping my legs in gunny sack, like puttees, held with twine; a habit I have always held to. Only dreams and memories were left to sustain the poverty and dreariness of my life. Now I was completely down.

But catastrophes never come singly and it was also that winter that the Matchless was again to be foreclosed. During a quarter of a century, the leases, the legal battles, the disappointments, the troubles and the finances of that mine had been one long series of involved ramifications. Each time the clouds would seems to have a silver lining, it would prove only a figment of my imagination or a mirage of the Cloud City (Leadville's nickname). A silver mine in the Cloud City should certainly have some lining!

"Why don't you give up? Let the mine go for the mortgage?" a Denver banker to whom I appealed for help said to me. "It's all worked out—and anyway it's paid you a small steady income for years."

"I should say not!" I replied with vehemence. "I shall never let the Matchless go—not while there is breath in my body to find a way to fight for it. The mine is a Golconda."

Doubting eyes greeted my statement and the money was refused. I was used to that—and in the quiet loneliness of my cabin or during my sombre meditations in church even I, too, occasionally doubted. Yet never would I let that be known. My great husband, Tabor, could not have spoken other than truthfully and prophetically from his deathbed and if I was to live true to his command, I must always believe.

"I have no reason for living if I do not have faith in the Matchless. No dear one is left to me. I have only this one legacy of my great love. It is my mission and my life," were the thoughts that ran through my head as I left the banker's office. But now I had exhausted my last resource. No future was ahead of me, no work to do and no place to live. The mine was doomed—and my heart sank to the lowest depths.

During that entire weekend, I wandered about Denver in a daze, telling my rosary in first one church and then another. About my neck, instead of beads, I always wore a long black shoelace knotted intermittently to form beads and holding a large plain wooden cross. Friends gave me other rosaries but I clung to my improvised string.

In some ways, my plain bedraggled habit, my make-shift rosary, my legs strapped in gunny sack and twine and my grey shawl over the black dress seemed only a just penance for the clothing extravagances and sins of my youth. I did not like to explain my attitude to most people—although I sometimes mentioned my feeling to friends or Fathers who were truly devout Catholics—but this thought gave me the courage to forget how I looked. Those rags were a chosen punishment for former vanity.

"Dear God, help me to save the Matchless," I prayed on my shoestring over and over again all day that Sunday. Suddenly as I knelt in St. Elizabeth's an inspiration came to me bathed in a white light. Gathering up my full skirt, I hurried from the church and headed toward the corner of Ninth and Pennsylvania Sts. and the home of J. K. Mullen. He was a millionaire miller and a liberal donor to many Catholic charities.

Outside in the night air it had begun to snow but I plodded on resolutely. By the time I had reached his dignified old mansion, it was past nine o'clock and I was afraid I should find no one home. But summoning a show of boldness, I rang the doorbell.

For a long time, there was no answer. I was cold and nervous, apart from my anxiety about the mine. I shifted my weight from one foot to another trying to make up my mind to ring again. At last I was sure enough to press the button. This time, after a short wait, the door slowly opened and revealed Mr. Mullen, himself.

"Good evening," I said pleasantly. "I'm Mrs. Tabor and I wondered if I might see you, although"—and laughed with that same musical laugh that had charmed so many illustrious men in its day—"it's a rather odd time for a call."

"Why, certainly, Mrs. Tabor, do come in. I'm all alone. And being Sunday night, the servants are all out—had to answer the door, myself."

He led me into a gloomy spacious room lit only by one reading lamp and by the flames from the fireplace.

"It's a pretty bad night for you to be out," he remarked.

"Oh, I don't mind. It's nothing to the Leadville blizzards I face all the time up at the mine. I'm used to a hard life."

"Well, you have a lot of courage."

"I need it—and it's taking a lot of courage to come here—but I'm depending on my cross,"—and I clasped it more tightly in my hand.

"What do you mean?"

Hesitantly I began to unfold my story to him. When I spoke of my loneliness and having only this one trust to live for, he remarked:

74

"Yes, I'm going through the same thing. You know, don't you, that **Mrs.** Mullen died last March? My daughters are all married and now I have nobody who really needs me."

"Oh, I'm deeply sorry."

We sat silent for some minutes, watching the fire and lost to our own thoughts. Finally Mr. Mullen urged me to go on. When I had finished my plea, he suddenly exclaimed:

"I will redeem that mortgage!"

Striding over to his desk, he sat down and wrote a check for $14,000 with the same impulsive generosity as W. S. Stratton had written his for $15,000 to Tabor in 1895.

"Oh, Mr. Mullen," I cried. "You are an angel!"

"Your story appealed to me, Mrs. Tabor, appealed to me very strongly. I think you deserve to keep the management of the Matchless."

My life and my mission were saved by a message straight from God!

Following up this action, in 1928, the J. K. Mullen estate created the Shorego Mining Co. and technically foreclosed the Matchless. But their action was to prevent other depredations and to preserve me from unfortunate business dealings. The Matchless has been really mine.

With the coming of the depression, gradually the owners and lessees abandoned the mines on Fryer Hill and the Matchless among them. Immediately after the pumps were stopped, the mines began to fill with water. Since many of the drifts are interlocking, today, in order to work the Matchless, not only its own shafts and drifts would have to be pumped dry but almost all of Fryer Hill, too. It has been a discouraging time, disappointments mounting one upon another.

I have had no income. Yet with my pride, I have never accepted charity. Where the least aspect of condescension could be imagined, I have returned gifts and refused offers of aid. But when I have been sure that people were genuinely friendly or would not speak about their generosity, I have let them help me, I have also received many donations through fan mail of late years— bills for $5, or $10 or even larger. These have come because of renewed interest in the Tabor name brought about by newspaper stories or by the book and movie, "Silver Dollar."

I read the book.

"It's all a pack of lies," I told anyone who asked me about it. But the story as a whole was more nearly right than I would care to admit especially considering its sneering tone. Of course, there are many inaccuracies like referring to Tabor as "Haw" (which no one ever called him in real life) and some straight geographical and historical untruths, such as having the Arkansas flow in Clear Creek Valley and talking of Central City as a collection of shanties when it is all brick or stone. The author was most unkind to me and talked about my guarding the mine with a shotgun, when in actuality I have never owned a shotgun that worked. It is true that I do not like strangers and I have several ways of dealing with them. If someone knocks, I peek out the corner of the window (which was once shaded by coarse lace, then burlap and finally newspapers), lifting just a tiny flap so as to show only one eye. If they see me and recognize me, I say I'm taking a bath—and I have been known to give that same answer all day long to a series of callers!

Sometimes I alter my voice and say, "Mrs. Tabor is downtown—I am the night watchman," (as I did when Sue Bonnie was making her first efforts to meet me) and sometimes I just sit as quiet as a mossy stone, pretending the cabin is uninhabited.

Nevertheless, the author of "Silver Dollar" did me a real service in bringing me many unseen friends and correspondents all across the United States. Carloads of people flock up Little Stray Horse Gulch each summer, seeking a glimpse of me, so many cars that I have renamed that road My Boulevard!

But I never speak to them or admit them to my cabin except, occasionally, when they come properly escorted by a Leadville friend. And when I go to town, I frequent the alleys as much as possible, my figure dressed in my long, black skirt and coat, my legs shrouded in burlap and twine and my face hidden by the perennial auto-cap with its visor and draping veil. I, who used to vaunt my public appearances in the streets by the most elegant dresses, matched by gay floating-ruffled parasols and by my liveried brougham and team, now skulk along beside the garbage cans and refuse.

When the movie "Silver Dollar" had its premiere in Denver late in 1932, the management approached me with an offer of cash and my expenses to Denver to be present. "No, I will not go," I replied firmly. "I can't leave the mine." (Actually I couldn't bear to see myself and all that I hold dear maligned.)

"I don't suppose you'd let us have some ore, then, from the Matchless? We want to have an historical exhibition in the foyer of everything we can get that relates to the Tabor mine."

"Certainly," I replied. "I'd be delighted. That's quite different. Tabor was a great miner and the Matchless is Colorado's most famous mine—naturally people will be interested."

I, myself, escorted the men out on the dump and helped them pick up a gunny sack full of the richest bits of ore we could find. When they had filled their sack, I waved them pleasantly on their way.

"Don't believe all you see," I said. "I'm not half as bad as in the book."

A couple of years later the motion picture came to Buena Vista and my friends, Joe Dewar and Lucille Frazier, asked me to motor down with them to see it. They were to keep our going a secret, I would wear a veil, dress differently than usual, and sit in the back of the theater so that no one would recognize me.

"That's a date, then," Joe said. "We'll be up for you Thursday evening."

But when Thursday arrived, I did not have the courage to go through with the plan. Here was I, a lonely, poverty-stricken old woman with only a sacred trust left to me out of all the world, a trust that most people spoke of as an 'obsession' or a 'fixation.' Yet now I must go to see what the world thought of me as a national beauty, a scandalous home-wrecker and a luxury-loving doll.

I could not face it. If I had sinned, I had paid a sufficiently high price for my sins without deliberately giving myself further heartache. I sent down a message to the village that I could not go.

Meanwhile, shortly after the premiere of the movie in Denver, I saw Father Horgan approaching with two men. When anybody knocked at my cabin, I always peeked out of the window to see who was there before admitting them. As I raised the burlap curtain sewed in heavy stitches of twine and recognized him, I asked:

"Whom have you got with you?"

"Two lawyers from Denver who want to talk to you about signing a paper— a business matter."

"Very well," I said. "Since *you* brought them—you know I don't like strangers. But I'll see them for your sake."

They entered and sat down in my humble quarters. I always kept the cabin very neat with a small shrine fastened to the far wall, my boxes, table and bed arranged around the room and the stove near the lean-to. It was December and very cold. They unfastened their coats and broached their offer by saying:

"How would you like to make $50,000?"

"You want to lease the Matchless?"

"No. We think your character has been damaged in the motion picture founded on your life and that you should sue for libel."

"But I haven't seen the movie—I can't testify to that—"

"Well, we have. And legally you have a very strong case."

So legally I had a very strong case? I knew something about litigation— my whole association with Tabor had been involved in law suits. Most of them, to be sure, were suits about mining claims but there was also the secret Durango divorce suit and the legal battle with Bill Bush. No good had ever come out of all that except fees to the lawyers—neither of us had gained anything in money or in reputation.

"But I do not need $50,000," I replied. "The Matchless will soon make many times that sum. But thank you very much indeed for your kindness and interest."

I turned to Father Horgan and introduced a discussion of religious matters with him. Shortly, however, the lawyers cut in again.

"But you could certainly use $50,000 extra. And all you have to do is put your name on this line."

They held out a paper already drawn up with an agreement for them to go ahead and sue in my name.

"But I'm not interested in the law. I'm interested in mining. To enter into such a business with you, I would have to learn many new things and I'm only interested in the price of silver, in high-grade ores and such like matters."

"You don't have to learn anything. Leave it all to us. We'll tend to everything."

"God will look after me. I put my trust in Him—not in men."

77

Each time they returned to the issue of obtaining my signature, I circumvented them in some such manner for I knew what that suit meant. It meant scandal. It meant the opposing side's digging back in the past and finding the name of Jacob Sands. There was not enough money in the world to pay me for besmirching the Tabor name, rightly or wrongly. But I did not hint at my real reasons for refusing. I merely turned to Father Horgan and asked him about another religious topic.

At last they became discouraged and took their departure. When I had said good-bye and closed the door, I stealthily opened it again, just a crack curiously wondering if I could hear any of their conversation. I only caught one comment as they went over the hill. One of the lawyers was saying to Father Horgan:

"Well, either that woman is the craziest woman in Colorado—or else she's the smartest!"

I closed the door and laughed merrily aloud.

"Indeed!" I exclaimed. "Well, I'm neither."

I was an old woman, living on stale bread that I bought twelve loaves at a time and plate boil which I bought in dollar lots. Plate boil is a brisquet part of the beef, like suet, and very, very cheap, at the same time that it generates heat. Lucille Frazier once asked me how I could bear to live on such a diet.

"Oh, I find it delectable," I answered, "really delectable."

That statement was not entirely true. But my dainty palate that used to have champagne and oysters whenever it wanted, had changed so much with the hardships of life that it no longer craved delicacies. My tongue had lost its taste for many sweetmeats and actually found this meagre unappetizing fare satisfying—and certainly more satisfying than to accept charity!

The Zaitz grocery kept me during these depression years in the necessary groceries at a very cheap rate or on credit. In addition, their delivery boys would often give me a lift from town to the cabin, sometimes breaking a trail through the snow for me.

When I was sick, never anything more than a cold, I would doctor myself with turpentine and lard, my favorite remedy for any ailment. And so I managed. If I did not have enough coal or wood to heat the cabin, I would go to bed for warmth. My Leadville friends generally kept an eye out for me and helped me surreptitiously through the worst crises. In these last years, there are many more friends than I could name.

So I have lived on—'existed on' would be a more correct statement. I have been lonely, blue, often cold and starving in the winters, and beset by many torments. But I have been sustained by a great faith and a great love. I have lived with courage and a cheery smile for my friends. As I look out over the abandoned shaft-houses and dumps of the fabulous Fryer Hill ruins, over the partially deserted town of Leadville to the glorious beauty of Colorado's highest mountains, I know that I have surely expiated my last sin and that I have fulfilled the trust my dear Tabor put in me when he said:

"Hang on to the Matchless."

Farewell

The last day anyone saw Mrs. Tabor alive was February 20, 1935. On that morning, she broke her way through deep snow around the Robert E. Lee mine which adjoined the Matchless on Fryer Hill, and walked the mile or more into the town of Leadville. Her old black dress was horribly torn and the twine and gunny sack wrappings on her feet were dripping wet because she had repeatedly fallen through the lowest snow crust into the melting freshets of running water beneath. The Zaitz delivery truck ran her home and let her out in Little Stray Horse Gulch beyond the abandoned railroad trestle (now gone), as close to the Matchless as it was possible to get. She walked off through the snow, carrying her bag of groceries and waving good-bye to the delivery boy, Elmer Kutzlub (now the owner of his own grocery store in Leadville).

Nothing more was known of her for two weeks although Sue Bonnie observed smoke issuing from her stack during some few days of that time. Then a fresh blizzard blew up, blotting out all vision for three days. When the storm cleared, Sue Bonnie, seeing from her own cabin on the outskirts of Leadville that Mrs. Tabor's stack was smokeless, became worried. She tried to reach her friend through the heavy fall of new snow but was not strong enough to make it. Sue had to wait until she could obtain help from Tom French to break a trail.

When they reached the cabin, all was silence. They broke a window and forced an entry. Mrs. Tabor's body, in the shape of a cross, was frozen stiff on the floor.

After the couple found Mrs. Tabor's emaciated form and her death was broadcast to the world, fourteen trunks of her earlier belongings turned up in a Denver warehouse and in the basement of St. Vincent's hospital in Leadville. But there was no other estate.

Burial posed a problem, both the question of place and the matter of expenses. But unsolicited donations poured into Leadville, sufficient to present a solution on both counts. The J. K. Mullen heirs, particularly the Oscar Malos, aided munificently. An interesting sidelight, during those days of indecision, was a bit of information given by Jim Corbett, the mortician, who said there were almost no grey hairs on her head. This corroborated Mrs. Tabor's claim that the one element of beauty left to her toward the end was her hair; for that reason she always wore the horrid motoring cap to hide it, punishing herself for the past.

Some weeks later, Baby Doe's body was shipped to Denver and buried in Mt. Olivet cemetery beside that of Horace Tabor who, in the meantime, had been moved from the now abandoned Calvary plot. At long last, after thirty-five years vigil, peace and reunion with her adored Tabor had come to Baby Doe's troubled soul.

And there, she rests today. On the edge of the plains where, a few miles beyond, the rampart of the Rockies bulks protectingly against the fair blue sky, little Lizzie McCourt of Oshkosh has found her final defense.

Despite the dazzling chapters and the story's consistent flamboyance, hers is a tragic tale. Although she epitomized a roistering era and a swashbuckling way of life made possible by the mining frontier of Colorado, the granite gloom of those powerful mountains has forever lowered the curtain on her dramatic period and on the valiant, if mistaken, spirit of Baby Doe Tabor. In relegating both, and their final evaluation, to the pages of history, the lines inscribed on the stage drop of the Tabor Opera House recur, ever again, emphasizing their fatal prophecy:

> *So fleet the works of men, back to the earth again,*
> *Ancient and holy things fade like a dream.*

Postscript :

Many years ago the first edition of this booklet appeared—on June 26, 1950. Five thousand copies sold in four months, and a second edition appeared before the end of the year. Since that time the editions have consisted of ten thousand copies each. The original edition was in the nature of a real gamble. In my mind the Tabor story had already received more than adequate attention in three books and countless articles, not to mention many fictional treatments and one movie. My work seemed rather supernumerary.

But this booklet had two virtues. In the other histories Baby Doe had been given the brush-off; as a floosy, when young, and a freak, when old. The other authors gave their sympathy to Augusta, and their research was not too painstaking. My booklet was based on what reporters call "leg-work." It was slow but it led me to an entirely different view of the second Mrs. Tabor and to a closer approximation of the probable truth. The general public liked my two contributions.

Among certain sectors, however, I was very much criticized for daring to defend Baby Doe and for writing fictional passages in this booklet for which I still have no proof. But oddly enough in some instances documentation later turned up for scenes that began as invention.

In 1956 the late John Latouche was chosen to write the libretto for an opera, *The Ballad of Baby Doe.* He read all available treatments of the Tabors but preferred this booklet (as he said in *Theatre Arts* magazine). His lyric telling of the story follows fairly closely the same line and found audiences across the United States and in Europe, where the opera has had a number of productions.

During the intervening years I have received fan mail from as far away as Yokohama, Japan, and Stuttgart, Germany, and the booklet continues to have wide appeal. It had been my intention to write a definitive large-size book on Baby Doe but I am not certain if there is sufficient interest for such a work. I should be glad to have the opinion of current readers.

80   Caroline Bancroft.